MARATHONER

What to Expect When Training for and Running a MARATHON

MARATHONER

What to Expect When Training for and Running a MARATHON

Matthew Huff

Illustrations by **Jason Kayser**
Photography by **Victor Sailer**
with Marathon History by **Bridget Quinn**

UNIVERSE

First published in the United States of America in 2021 by
Universe Publishing
A Division of Rizzoli International Publications, Inc.
300 Park Avenue South
New York, NY 10010
www.rizzoliusa.com

All photographs © Victor Sailer, except for the following:

p. 36: © Danny Baca & Natalie Morris; p. 48: © Thomas Hollaender/Shutterstock.com; p. 52: © Ari Scott;
p. 54: © Drew Reynolds; p. 56: © GH Studio/Shutterstock.com; p. 62: © Lauren Trost; p. 70: © Rich Yee;
p. 72: © Baloncici/Shutterstock.com; p. 77: © Tiffany Renshaw; p. 86: © Galen Dow; p. 119: Courtesy of George Hirsch;
p. 122: © ZamoraA/iStockphoto.com; p. 126: © Humphrey Oleng; p. 170: © Carol Mast Beach; p. 171: Courtesy of Dave Obelkevich;
p. 174: © skynesher/iStockphoto.com; pp. 184 & 185: Courtesy of Kate Carter; p. 198: Courtesy of Bank of America Chicago Marathon;
p. 206: © Da Ping Luo/New York Road Runners via Getty Images; and pp. 208–209: © Sgt. Michael S. Cifuentes/USMC.

Publisher: Charles Miers (Virginia Beach Marathon, 2:16:37, 1988 Olympic Trials qualifier)
Associate Publisher: James Muschett (Marine Corps Marathon, 3:28:17)
Managing Editor: Lynn Scrabis (Pittsburgh Marathon, 4:13:56)
Editor: Candice Fehrman
Design: Lori Malkin Ehrlich
Text: Matthew Huff (Houston Marathon, 3:45:08)
Photography: Victor Sailer (New York City Marathon, 3:41:55)
Illustrations: Jason Kayser

Disclaimer: Running is a strenuous form of exercise. Always seek the advice of your physician or other qualified
health professional before starting or changing any exercise program or making a lifestyle change.

All interviews in this book have been condensed and edited for clarity and brevity.

To learn more, please follow author Matthew Huff (@huffmatt) on Twitter and Instagram.

Printed in China

2021 2022 2023 2024 / 10 9 8 7 6 5 4 3 2 1

ISBN: 978-0-7893-3971-3

Library of Congress Control Number: 2020945553

Visit us online:
Facebook.com/RizzoliNewYork
Twitter: @Rizzoli_Books
Instagram.com/RizzoliBooks
Pinterest.com/RizzoliBooks
Youtube.com/user/RizzoliNY
Issuu.com/Rizzoli

Pages 2–3: Paris Marathon, France, 2007
Pages 6–7: Athens Marathon, Greece, 2012

To Mimi and Papa,
for teaching me about carb-loading, power napping,
and the rejuvenating force of reality TV

LYLYLY

▼▼▼

CONTENTS

Prerace

Welcome to *Marathoner*! When I think of this 26.2-mile behemoth of a race, I keep thinking of two quotations I accumulated while writing this book. The first is from Michal Kapral, who won the Toronto Marathon in 2002: "I love the idea of pushing yourself to the limit because that's how I always ran. I never felt like I had much raw talent, but I felt like I could out-suffer people. That's how the marathon appealed to me. It's a great distance to suffer." Cheery, right?

Running a marathon is certainly a difficult and painful endeavor. If you sign up for a race thinking anything else, then you are in for a rude awakening. Over the months of training for and finally running a marathon, you will encounter all sorts of feelings and experiences you didn't know were possible, and most of them won't be pleasant. The marathon is a masochist's sport.

The second quotation is from Boston Marathon winner and journalist Amby Burfoot, who told me marathons aren't about winning or losing (only one person wins, and most likely it won't be you). Instead, he said, "It's about everyday people doing extraordinary things with their lives—finishing marathons, and losing weight, and getting in shape, and going to graduate school, and surviving divorce, and the infinite number of stories that are out there."

Marathons are about overcoming. We don't run marathons because they're easy. We run them because they're a nightmare to get through, but by finishing them we prove to ourselves that we will not be defeated by adversity. We prove to ourselves that by surviving this pain maybe we can survive other pains. We prove that we are resilient, that we cannot be stopped, that we are stronger than we thought we were. So, who's ready? Let's get running!

<< Tokyo Marathon, Japan, 2009

26 Marathon Training Tips

There are countless books dedicated solely to marathon training: detailed schedules of exactly how long to run and when and at what speeds, what stretches and exercises to do on off days, what foods you should be eating and in what quantities, and precisely how to best use your foam roller. Unfortunately, we've got limited space here, but if you want my day-by-day training schedule or my guacamole recipe, feel free to send me a private message via social media. I do, however, have some tips for you. Here are 26. That's one for every mile.

☐ **1: Commit to running the marathon.** Meb Keflezighi says, "We all have trouble getting out the door, so lacing up the shoes for everyone is hard, but if you commit, you will excel no matter what."

☐ **2: Download a training calendar.** Depending on your experience level, you will want more or less lead time to train. In general, all training is the same, with one progressively longer run each week, as well as two to four shorter runs.

☐ **3: Start with the shoes.** People love to buy running gadgets, but rather than purchasing a fancy watch right away, get the shoes and start training. Once you've been running for a bit, you'll have a better idea as to exactly which accoutrements you need.

☐ **4: Cross train.** Having a strong, fit body will help you stay healthy and uninjured on long runs. Core strength is especially important.

☐ **5: Stretch.** It goes without saying, but . . .

☐ **6: Put Beyoncé on your playlist.** She is a motivator.

☐ **7: Get used to uncomfortable.** The sooner you realize this is going to be difficult, the better off you'll be.

☐ **8: Set aside time for those long runs.** Put them all on your calendar now so you can schedule around them. Skipping long runs is the fastest route to failure.

☐ **9: Run with a marathoner.** Ryan Hall says, "For first-time marathoners, I think it's important to train with people who have run marathons. That way you can get confidence from knowing that you're training with people who have done what you're trying to do."

☐ **10: Don't run with a concussion (or really any injury).** If you hit your head getting off a bus, don't run a marathon. I can tell you from personal experience. The same goes for knee, ankle, hip, and back injuries. Take a break and recover. Running a race is not worth it.

☐ **11: Have a hydration strategy.** Either know where you can get water on long runs or bring a water bottle with you. We don't want you passing out on us.

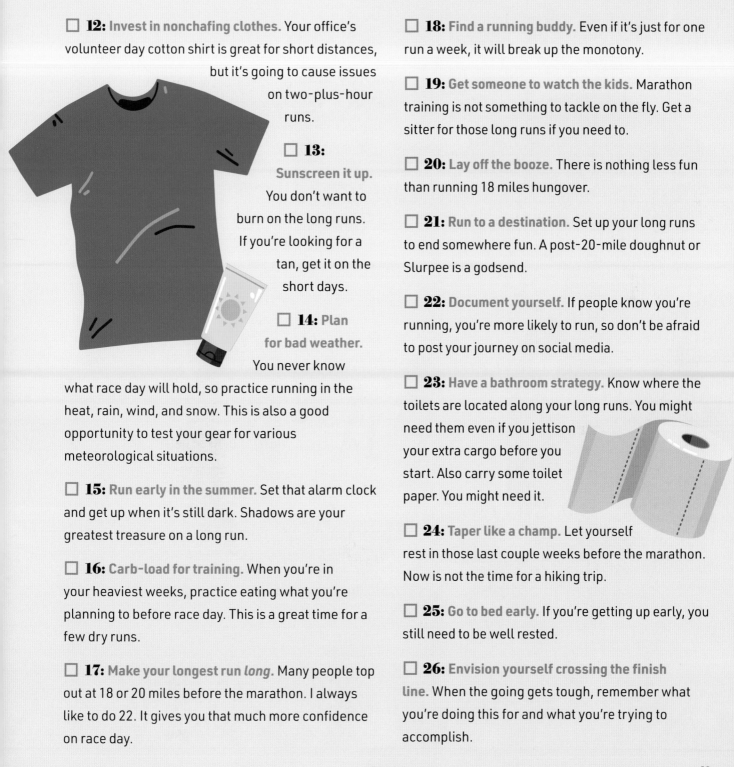

☐ **12:** **Invest in nonchafing clothes.** Your office's volunteer day cotton shirt is great for short distances, but it's going to cause issues on two-plus-hour runs.

☐ **13:** **Sunscreen it up.** You don't want to burn on the long runs. If you're looking for a tan, get it on the short days.

☐ **14:** **Plan for bad weather.** You never know what race day will hold, so practice running in the heat, rain, wind, and snow. This is also a good opportunity to test your gear for various meteorological situations.

☐ **15:** **Run early in the summer.** Set that alarm clock and get up when it's still dark. Shadows are your greatest treasure on a long run.

☐ **16:** **Carb-load for training.** When you're in your heaviest weeks, practice eating what you're planning to before race day. This is a great time for a few dry runs.

☐ **17:** **Make your longest run *long*.** Many people top out at 18 or 20 miles before the marathon. I always like to do 22. It gives you that much more confidence on race day.

☐ **18:** **Find a running buddy.** Even if it's just for one run a week, it will break up the monotony.

☐ **19:** **Get someone to watch the kids.** Marathon training is not something to tackle on the fly. Get a sitter for those long runs if you need to.

☐ **20:** **Lay off the booze.** There is nothing less fun than running 18 miles hungover.

☐ **21:** **Run to a destination.** Set up your long runs to end somewhere fun. A post-20-mile doughnut or Slurpee is a godsend.

☐ **22:** **Document yourself.** If people know you're running, you're more likely to run, so don't be afraid to post your journey on social media.

☐ **23:** **Have a bathroom strategy.** Know where the toilets are located along your long runs. You might need them even if you jettison your extra cargo before you start. Also carry some toilet paper. You might need it.

☐ **24:** **Taper like a champ.** Let yourself rest in those last couple weeks before the marathon. Now is not the time for a hiking trip.

☐ **25:** **Go to bed early.** If you're getting up early, you still need to be well rested.

☐ **26:** **Envision yourself crossing the finish line.** When the going gets tough, remember what you're doing this for and what you're trying to accomplish.

Which Marathon Should You Run?

With more than 800 marathons held annually around the world, you've got a ton of options when it comes to earning that 26.2 bumper sticker. So which race should you sign up for? Here are some things to consider as you make your choice.

■ **Easy Access:** Home-field advantage is real. Picking a marathon close to home (especially for your first) can be a huge boost. Sleep in your own bed the night before, banish all those travel anxieties, and train on similar terrain to the race. Most importantly, you can easily guilt every person you know into cheering for you.

■ **Barrier to Entry:** Major marathons (New York, Chicago, London) have more applicants than places for runners, so you've got to win a lottery (or raise a ton of money for charity) in order to enter. You'll need to plan ahead to get into one of these. Boston is even trickier because you have to qualify with a *very* fast time in a previous marathon.

■ **Trail vs. Road:** While road races are more popular, trail marathons are growing. With more difficult terrain, less course support, and fewer runners, these races require additional training, so don't sign up unless you've spent some time running trails. They do, however, offer more nature and none of those dreaded highway stretches.

■ **Price:** Yes, you do have to pay for the torture of running a marathon, and in some cases you must pay a pretty penny. The 2019 New York City Marathon, for example, cost $295 to run ($358 for non-US residents). Meanwhile, smaller marathons, like the City of Trees Marathon in Boise, Idaho, costs as little as $68 depending on when you sign up. Virtual races are even cheaper (see page 189 for more information).

■ **Time of Year:** With around three months of training recommended, choosing a marathon by race date is common. Spring marathons require training in the cold, while fall marathons mean you're running in August. Marathons in summer or winter are rarer, but you can find one every weekend of the year.

■ **Weather:** If you're trying to avoid the heat or rain or cold, choose a more temperate marathon. Most races include typical weather forecasts on their websites, so you can plan ahead. For more information on race-day weather, see the chapter starting on page 95.

■ **The Goodies:** Many middle-tier marathons seek to differentiate themselves with their swag. Scope out Instagram to see which races dole out the biggest medals, best participant tees, or fun extras.

■ **Fans:** Cheering crowds are a huge motivating force—especially in the back half of a marathon—so picking a race known for its roadside supporters is a perk.

<< *Clockwise from top left: Venice Marathon, Italy, 2009; San Francisco Marathon, California, USA, 2017; Tokyo Marathon, Japan, 2009; Philadelphia Marathon, Pennsylvania, USA, 2006; Toronto Marathon, Canada, 2015; Antarctica Marathon, Antarctica, 1997* **Page 17:** *Berlin Marathon, Germany, 2006*

"Over the months of training for a marathon, you will encounter all sorts of feelings and experiences you didn't know were possible."

Marathon Morning

The predawn hours before the blast of the airhorn were created solely for worrying. For months, you have meticulously trained for these 26.2 miles, but sometime in the middle of the night, while you were sleeping (because a well-rested body is a strong body), the reality set in. All of that training could go down the drain if you make a misstep in your last hours of prerace prep. Do the right things, however, and your future self will thank you.

First up, food. Eating too much can lead to cramps (or, worse, puking), but eating too little can leave you flagging well before the finish. Veteran marathon pacer Jim Crist suggests taking in 500 to 600 calories as soon as you wake up so the food is digested by the time you hit the starting line. Then eat a snack (granola bar or banana) an hour before the start. Get a good mix of carbs and protein (you'll see a lot of peanut butter bagels on marathoning blogs), and steer clear of anything your body isn't used to. There's no need to try a new breakfast burrito and spend half of the race in port-o-john lines.

Hydrate on a similar schedule. Drink a big ol' glass of water when you wake up (say three to four hours before the start), and sip on a Gatorade while you're on the way to the starting line. To prevent a sloshy stomach and early bathroom breaks, though, avoid chugging fluids in the immediate runup to the race.

Before you head for the start, you also need to get your gear and clothes in order. Apply sunscreen, and lather antichafing balm or Vaseline on your thighs or armpits to prevent friction. Men, you also need to tape or lubricate your nipples to avoid a tandem of scarlet letters soaking through your shirt.

Consult your weather app one last time and decide what to wear. Keep in mind that you can always take layers off, but unless you plan to make a pit stop at Gap midmarathon you can't add layers. Wearing raggedy old sweatshirts or garbage bags can be a good solution if it's a cold morning; you can stay warm while you're waiting for the gun and then ditch them once you're warmed up. Marathon workers will pick up whatever you leave behind, but you might not want to part with your $200 Under Armour hoodie.

Don't tie your shoes too tight (extra blisters) or too loose (tendon nightmare). Don't forget your bib. Don't forget your gels. Don't forget your gear-check bag, water bottle, ankle brace, or headphones (if the race allows them). Whatever got you through those training runs is what you'll want with you for the actual race.

And, most important of all, don't forget to poop. Bowel movement anxiety is the paramount stress of all marathoners. Waiting in line for a dank port-o-john at Mile 12 that 50 other racers have already, er, borrowed, is every racer's nightmare. You lose time, you lose momentum, your body gets stiff. So instead spend some time prerun jettisoning all waste from your body.

Most races request that you arrive to the start an hour early, even earlier if there is security, which gives you plenty of time to stretch before the start. It also gives you plenty of time to worry. Did you train enough? How are

26 + 1 Marathons to Run

Caught the marathon bug and looking for more races to run? Here's a bucket list of some of the greatest marathons around the globe each year. From the world majors and big-city street races to international adventures and my favorite small-town events, I've got you covered. Here's one for each mile and an extra as a treat.

WORLD MAJORS

1. **Berlin Marathon**
   Berlin, Germany
2. **Boston Marathon**
   Boston, Massachusetts
3. **Chicago Marathon**
   Chicago, Illinois
4. **London Marathon**
   London, United Kingdom
5. **New York City Marathon**
   New York City, New York
6. **Tokyo Marathon**
   Tokyo, Japan

US RACES

7. **Atlanta Marathon**
   Atlanta, Georgia
8. **Big Sur Marathon**
   Big Sur, California
9. **Detroit Marathon**
   Detroit, Michigan
10. **Hatfield-McCoy Marathon**
    South Williamson, Kentucky
11. **Houston Marathon**
    Houston, Texas
12. **Los Angeles Marathon**
    Los Angeles, California
13. **Marine Corps Marathon**
    Washington, DC
14. **Portland Marathon**
    Portland, Oregon
15. **Twin Cities Marathon**
    Minneapolis and St. Paul, Minnesota
16. **Vermont City Marathon**
    Burlington, Vermont

INTERNATIONAL RACES

17. **Athens Marathon**
    Athens, Greece
18. **Great Ocean Road Marathon**
    Victoria, Australia
19. **Great Wall Marathon**
    Tianjin, China
20. **Inca Trail Marathon**
    Cusco, Peru
21. **Lewa Safari Marathon**
    Lewa Downs, Kenya
22. **Midnight Sun Marathon**
    Tromsø, Norway
23. **Paris Marathon**
    Paris, France
24. **Petra Desert Marathon**
    Petra, Jordan
25. **Rotterdam Marathon**
    Rotterdam, Netherlands
26. **Toronto Waterfront Marathon**
    Toronto, Canada

AND FINALLY . . .

27. **Your Hometown Marathon!**

you going to tackle that hill at Mile 22? Will you beat your personal record? Should you run with the pace group? Did you feel a weird twinge in your knee? Should you try to "go" one last time?

You will hear the race announcers thanking sponsors and the mayor saying things like, "You couldn't have asked for better weather," but that's all in the background. Mostly you'll just want the airhorn to sound. Every marathon is a mystery until you start. Some troubles will arise. Most will not. But the only way to find out is to run.

How Are You Getting to the Starting Line?

Yeah, sure, the 26.2 is a big deal, but the journey to the starting line can be the stuff of harrowing legend as well. Start times are early, parking is a nightmare, and all the while you're fretting over the schedule of your, er, guts. So I'm going to help you out. Here is your step-by-step guide to the race before the race.

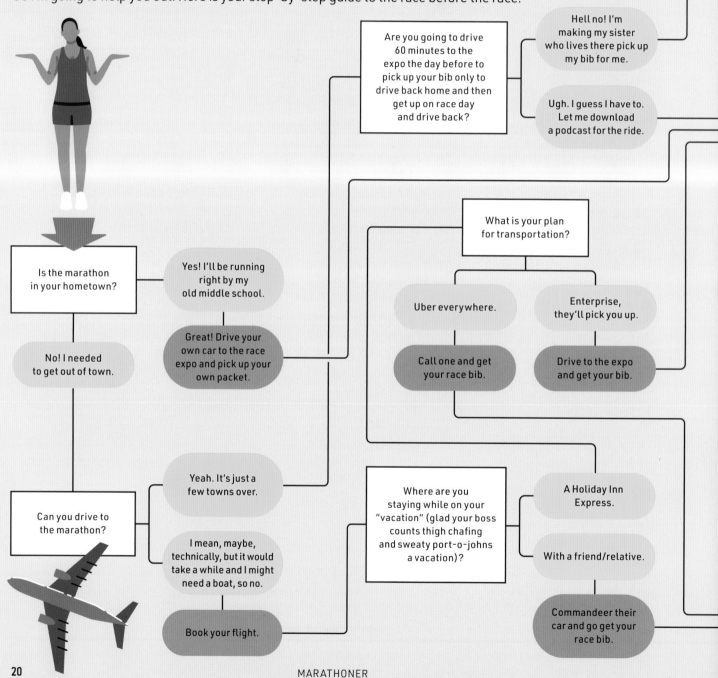

Are you going to drive 60 minutes to the expo the day before to pick up your bib only to drive back home and then get up on race day and drive back?

Hell no! I'm making my sister who lives there pick up my bib for me.

Ugh. I guess I have to. Let me download a podcast for the ride.

What is your plan for transportation?

Uber everywhere.

Call one and get your race bib.

Enterprise, they'll pick you up.

Drive to the expo and get your bib.

Is the marathon in your hometown?

Yes! I'll be running right by my old middle school.

Great! Drive your own car to the race expo and pick up your own packet.

No! I needed to get out of town.

Can you drive to the marathon?

Yeah. It's just a few towns over.

I mean, maybe, technically, but it would take a while and I might need a boat, so no.

Book your flight.

Where are you staying while on your "vacation" (glad your boss counts thigh chafing and sweaty port-o-johns a vacation)?

A Holiday Inn Express.

With a friend/relative.

Commandeer their car and go get your race bib.

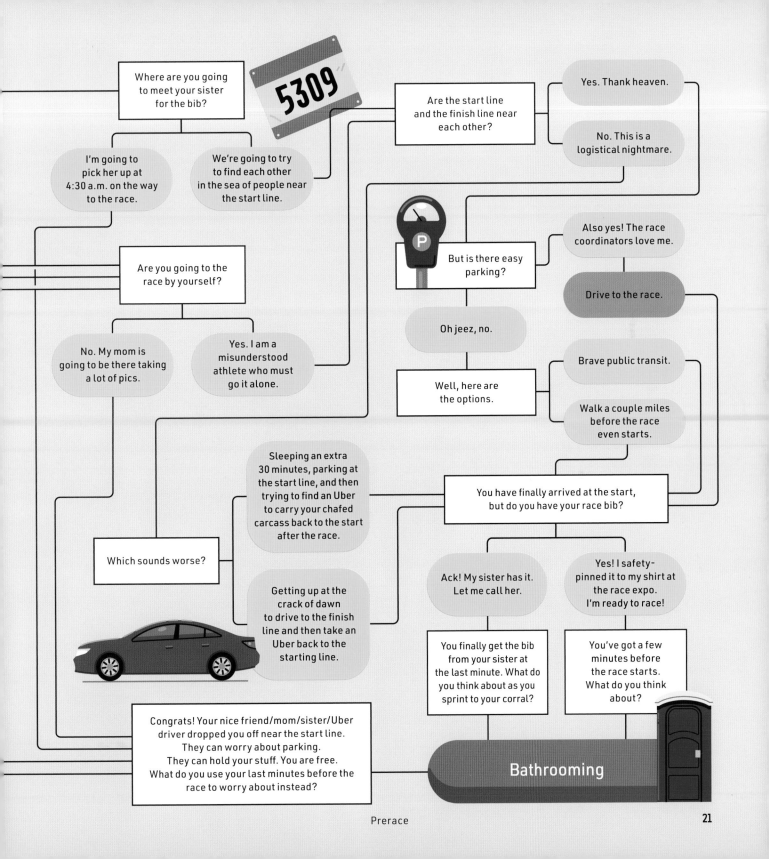

Where are you going to meet your sister for the bib?

5309

I'm going to pick her up at 4:30 a.m. on the way to the race.

We're going to try to find each other in the sea of people near the start line.

Are the start line and the finish line near each other?

Yes. Thank heaven.

No. This is a logistical nightmare.

Are you going to the race by yourself?

But is there easy parking?

Also yes! The race coordinators love me.

Drive to the race.

No. My mom is going to be there taking a lot of pics.

Yes. I am a misunderstood athlete who must go it alone.

Oh jeez, no.

Well, here are the options.

Brave public transit.

Walk a couple miles before the race even starts.

Sleeping an extra 30 minutes, parking at the start line, and then trying to find an Uber to carry your chafed carcass back to the start after the race.

You have finally arrived at the start, but do you have your race bib?

Which sounds worse?

Ack! My sister has it. Let me call her.

Yes! I safety-pinned it to my shirt at the race expo. I'm ready to race!

Getting up at the crack of dawn to drive to the finish line and then take an Uber back to the starting line.

You finally get the bib from your sister at the last minute. What do you think about as you sprint to your corral?

You've got a few minutes before the race starts. What do you think about?

Congrats! Your nice friend/mom/sister/Uber driver dropped you off near the start line. They can worry about parking. They can hold your stuff. You are free. What do you use your last minutes before the race to worry about instead?

Bathrooming

MILE 1

Happy Crowds

The starting gun blasts, and you're off! The marathon—the crowning athletic achievement of most runners' lives—is a fleet of feet pounding the pavement with the masses on the way to the 26.2, the medal, and the bragging rights.

Mile 1 is a deceptively charming place. Look left. Look right. Take in your fellow runners, giddy to be embarking on their long journey toward the finish line. With the fans hollering encouragement, Mile 1 resembles the early scene in *Titanic* during which the folks on the boat are waving to the people on dry land. Everyone is smiling, and no one is prepared for the carnage to come.

Maneuvering Mile 1 primarily consists of crowd control. The start is jam-packed, and you'll need to weave around groups of slow joggers in matching T-shirts while trying not to get run over by the cross-country superstars, practically hurdling other racers on their way to a three-hour finish.

You'll also need to avoid the strippers. On cold mornings, runners milling around the start wear anything to keep warm: sweatshirts, garbage bags, ponchos, blankets, even burlap sacks. After five minutes of excited running, however, racers are warm and ready to ditch their old sorority crewnecks. Mile 1 is an obstacle course of flying jackets and elbows. Duck to avoid a black eye.

Aside from dodging other runners and their discarded vestments (it all gets donated to charity, by the way), you'll wish Mile 1 would last longer—the good tidings, the adoring well-wishers, the knee injury that hasn't started aching yet, the hill at Mile 20 still way out in the future. This is where you can still smile, feel your toes, and give the crowd a good wave.

<< *Chicago Marathon, Illinois, USA, 2008* **Pages 23–24:** *Boston Marathon, Massachusetts, USA, 2011*

Famous Mile 1s

■ Want to be serenaded by country singers during your first mile? Look no further than the Rock 'n' Roll Nashville Marathon, which starts on the city's famous Broadway, home to dozens of honky-tonk bars. Countless famous country stars got their start on this strip, and Nashville's premier running event decided it would as well.

■ The New York City Marathon, one of the Abbott World Marathon Majors, prides itself on sending runners through all five of the Big Apple's boroughs. The race spends all of 10 seconds in Staten Island before heading toward Brooklyn via the Verrazzano-Narrows Bridge with a beautiful morning view of New York Harbor.

■ If you don't mind trekking hundreds of miles into the Australian bush, you can enjoy views of the massive red-rock formation Uluru/Ayers Rock during the first mile of the Australian Outback Marathon.

■ There is no more important first mile of a marathon than that of the Athens Marathon. Starting at the sport's namesake—Marathon, Greece—runners begin by tracing the steps of Pheidippides, the event's first participant. According to legend, he died upon arrival, but he felt good in Marathon and you will too.

MARATHON VOCAB WORD

corral: a holding area for a specific group of runners prior to the marathon's start

In order to prevent mass pandemonium at the start of large races, runners are separated into corrals, each of which is released individually in a staggered start. Corrals are usually organized by prospective finish times, with the "I'm trying to win" runners in the first corral and the "I'm just trying to survive" runners toward the back. Ideally, runners are grouped with people who run at the same pace, so the crowded early miles aren't riddled with runners making potentially dangerous moves while jockeying for position. There are often also separate corrals for handcyclists, elite runners, and half-marathoners. Typically, the larger the marathon, the more corrals (small marathons might not have them at all). Prior to the race, entrants are assigned their corral, which their bib will typically also identify. The corrals are usually marked with signs bearing either a number or letter (Corral J, Corral 14) or a mile pace (8:30, 9:00, etc.). Some races (like the Walt Disney World Marathon) heavily police the corrals, while others (like the Baltimore Marathon) use the corrals as more of a suggestion. In either case, getting an early corral comes with bragging rights.

"Some idiot put me in Corral J, which is ridiculous because I could run a mean 100m back in high school."

✔ BODY CHECK – Ideal Body Prep

For many runners, the marathon is the most physically grueling feat they'll endure in their entire lives. With that in mind, your body needs to be at its *best* at the starting line. Sure, this means making good choices on marathon morning, but also in the days leading up to the race. Get plenty of sleep. It can be tough to sleep the night before (nerves!), so stockpile the Zs (when hopefully you're less nervous). As with sleep, make sure to drink plenty of water and eat lots of nutritious foods. Overhydrating and binge eating in the 12 hours before a marathon can leave you bloated and sluggish, so make sure to eat and drink thoughtfully for the week prior. Checking the color of your pee can be a good way to make sure you're hydrated. Clear means all systems go; gold means drink more. With food, make sure you're getting plenty of protein (grilled chicken, peanut butter, eggs) and carbs (pasta, toast, potatoes). You may be tempted to eat salads and fruit in the lead-up because they are traditionally considered "healthier," but those aren't going to give you as much energy in the race. And, of course, don't start trying spicy or exotic new foods three days before your marathon. Running 26 miles with an upset stomach would not be fun.

The standard piece of advice touted even by nonrunners is to carb-load the night before the marathon. While carbs are a great source for the energy your body will need during the race, eating too much the night before can simply mean you're hauling around extra cargo, especially if your body isn't used to digesting Olive Garden's Tour of Italy. For plenty more advice on food, see the chapter starting on page 73.

Bonus points go to runners who also stretch and stay off their feet in the days leading up to the race. There's no need for sore ankles or stiff thighs before the race starts. Your goal is to cross that starting line without a hint of tiredness, hunger, stiffness, or thirst because you'll face all of those challenges on the path to the finish. And speaking of the finish, save the beers for after the race as well. ◼

The history of the marathon dates back to 490 BCE, when an Athenian herald named (maybe) Pheidippides is said to have raced some 25 miles from the coastal village of Marathon to the city-state of Athens. He was running to announce the unlikely victory of the outnumbered Athenian forces over an invading Persian army, an event better known to history as the Battle of Marathon, a pivotal little skirmish that saved democracy and led to the rise of classical civilization. No wonder Pheidippides is said to have exclaimed upon reaching Athens, "Rejoice! We conquer!" before dropping dead from exhaustion. Cue endless jibes from nonrunners about the perils of marathons. Though contemporary historians think it's unlikely Pheidippides made the Marathon-to-Athens run (he may have done a far longer, mountainous run from Athens to Sparta and back again), or died as a result, the point is that romantic Europeans later believed it was true.

*To provide a little historical context on the marathon, a race that has been around for 2,500 years, I recruited my friend **Bridget Quinn** (hereafter **BQ**). A writer, runner, and historian, BQ will be popping up from time to time to share the wildest, weirdest, and most foundational moments from marathons past.*

■ ■ ■ ■

Running along with Marathon Legend *Meb Keflezighi*

You can't write a book about marathons in the United States without discussing Meb Keflezighi, the only runner in history to win the New York City Marathon, the Boston Marathon, and an Olympic medal in the marathon. The Eritrean-born runner brought new life to the sport in America during his prolific career and 26 runnings of the 26.2. Despite his initial protests that he was just "a miler," he tacked on distance until 2002, when during an Olympic off year (he ran the 10,000M in 2000 in his first of four appearances at the games), he decided to "give it a shot" in New York. Here's what he has to say about first marathons, first miles, and the first time he ran a race with food poisoning.

You ended up finishing ninth in your first marathon. How did you feel at the end?
I finished 2:12:35, which is 35 seconds shy of the A Standard for the Olympics [a cutoff time dictating who qualifies for the Olympic Trials and how many athletes a country can send]. Physically, I was devastated. Emotionally, I was like, "No way. There's nothing in this. What's the fun in this?" I said, "This is ridiculous." I couldn't walk. I was cold and chilly. When I finished, I was defeated. You can defeat the marathon sometimes, but it can also defeat you. I was defeated by it.

So what ultimately made you come back?
Two weeks later, I went back to Eritrea, where I was born, with my mom for the first time since 1986. I saw how people live in the village with no electricity and no running water. I said, "You know what? I guess I got no room to complain. Nobody put a gun to my head and said you have to do a marathon." It was something I wanted to do, and I loved it for the first 16 or 17 miles. When I came back [my coach Bob Larsen] said, "Why do you want to do it again?" I told him how people were working from sunrise to sunset with no choice but to survive. I said, "This is a personal choice and I want to do it." I did the Chicago Marathon. It's the only race I didn't go for the win. I just ran to break 2:12, and I ran 2:10:03, and I said, "This can be cool."

Let's talk about the beginning of a marathon. What is running through your mind in the minutes before the gun goes off?
You're thinking, "Is the body going to make it?" You're thinking, "Can I finish this race?" But you have to believe. There's nothing you can do. You can overthink it. You have to think, "I'm here. How fortunate am I to be here now? I'm healthy. I'm strong. I'm going to go."

Do you have any prerace rituals?

I just make sure I double tie my shoes. I make sure I have my electrolytes. I make sure I have my ChapStick, which I have in my shoe usually before the race. I take it out, put the ChapStick on, and hopefully go for it.

What are your strategies for Mile 1?

The beauty of running the marathon is that I don't have to sprint. I just have to pace myself. The first few miles are very low-key. Especially in New York or Boston, you just need composure. Calm down. Relax. Let your body warm up. It's irrelevant what splits you run on those courses. Just make sure you fight for your spot at the beginning, so you don't get tripped.

What was your worst marathon experience?

One was the 2006 New York City Marathon, where I had food poisoning. I did everything right, and I thought, "I've been second place, I've been third place, I'm ready for the win." I got food poisoning, and my luggage never made it to me on a direct flight, which is strange. But I said, "I'm here, and I'm going to do whatever I need to get ready because I've been training for three to four months with this one goal in mind. Food poisoning or not, I'm going to go for it." I went out halfway in the lead, but then the food poisoning thing caught up to me. All those things went wrong, but I still finished the marathon.

Now that you're retired professionally, what does your relationship with the marathon look like?

I've done two marathons since I retired. I like to run for the Meb Foundation. I like to give out medals at the finish line, or surprise people in the middle of the course and give them high fives and encourage them to keep going strong. I always encourage people to run one marathon in their lifetime. After that, it's optional.

"*Mile One . . . everyone is smiling, and no one is prepared for the carnage to come.*"

Starting-Line Traditions

Starting guns and foghorns are so blasé. With more than 1,000 marathons run in the United States alone each year, some races are finding more creative ways of releasing their runners. The Marine Corps Marathon, run every October in Washington, DC, begins its race with tandem paratroopers carrying the American flag toward the Pentagon before the starting gun. In Orlando, the Walt Disney World Marathon begins with Mickey and Minnie setting off a shower of fireworks. The Air Force Marathon begins with a flyover; the Chickamauga Battlefield Marathon blasts off a Civil War–era cannon; and racers in the Rome Marathon were once sent out by a prayer from the Pope.

Perhaps the grandest marathon start comes at the Rock 'n' Roll Las Vegas Marathon, where runners enjoy an evening concert (Macklemore and Ryan Lewis performed in 2014) before they set off through the bright lights of the Vegas Strip. In a slightly more low-key (but no less amusing) ceremony, actors dressed up as feuding patriarchs shoot a shotgun in a grocery store parking lot to begin the Hatfield-McCoy Marathon in South Williamson, Kentucky. Meanwhile, Boston is still just shooting blanks.

First Assessments

Welcome to Mile 2! One mile down! Only 25 and change to go!

While Mile 1 is pure distraction and easy to get caught up in, by Mile 2 the crowds have thinned a little and runners are finding their rhythm. You've been running for a good 10 or 15 minutes, and your body has intuited that you are not sprinting away from a rogue mugger. Now is the time for your first full-body inventory.

Anyone who has ever run for exercise (New Year's resolution gym goers, this includes you) knows that you have good days and bad days. During your months of marathon training, you trucked through 18-mile runs that left you saying, "I could do more," and you panted through five-mile runs. You weren't sick or tired or going through a breakup, but for whatever reason (voodoo curse? bad karma? low sodium intake?) running just felt hard. And that, boys and girls, is the stuff of marathoning nightmares. What if, after months of training, you start running and your race day is also a bad day?

Of course, the marathon is a long race (eight hours long for some!), so a lot can change between now and the finish. Races have been won by people who felt cruddy at Mile 2, and Lord knows front-runners at this point rarely win, but finally being able to assess your situation is a relief either way. For better or worse, this is what your body feels like. Now you know and can start making a battle plan for the next 24 miles.

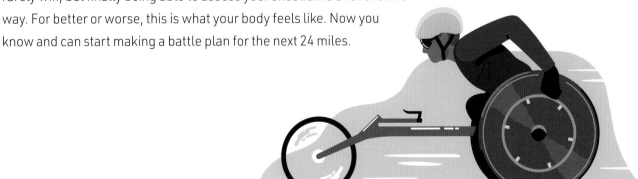

<< Prague Marathon, Czech Republic, 2015

✔ BODY CHECK – Adrenaline and Endorphins

So, you're feeling good at Mile 2. Perhaps too good. The culprit? The dastardly duo of adrenaline and endorphins. Adrenaline, the hormone responsible for our fight-or-flight instinct, is triggered when we're stressed, excited, or nervous (sound like feelings you'd have at the start of a marathon?) and gives us energy to fend off attackers. Endorphins are hormones our bodies release during exercise that diminish our perception of pain and trigger positive feelings (think healthy, natural morphine). As you can see, the nerves runners experience before a race produce adrenaline, which gives you energy to run, which in turn produces endorphins. By Mile 2, you've got both hormones pumping through your system, telling your brain you feel awesome! While this euphoria is great in the moment, it will wear off in the course of four hours of running, and you'll have to finish the marathon without these chemicals driving you forward. Enjoy this early high, but don't run too fast too soon because once these pesky little chemicals vanish, you could be in for a world of hurt. ■

HALFMARATHON 2782

8236 MARATHON

MARATHON VOCAB WORD

bib: a piece of paper with an identifying number and information, issued by race organizers to each participant in a marathon, to be worn during the race

In addition to displaying your race number, which is used for registration and tracking purposes (as well as identifying you in photos), the bib also differentiates between paying race entrants and illegal runners. If you don't have a bib, security can send you packing. Bibs—usually made of tearproof and waterproof (i.e., sweatproof and Gatorade-proof) paper—are attached to runners' shirts or shorts with safety pins. They also often contain electronic strips used for tracking race times, are printed with your corral assignment, and are color-coded by event (marathon, half-marathon, relay, etc.). In the Detroit Marathon, first-time marathoners are given easily recognizable green bibs and are called "Greenies."

"I got passed by an old man at Mile 18, but he had on a relay bib, so I didn't feel as bad."

Running with a Companion

They say misery loves company, and there is no more miserable place than a marathon. So, should you run with a friend? Here are the pros and cons of running by yourself or with others.

	PROS	CONS
Going It Alone	■ You run at your own pace on your own schedule. ■ There's plenty of time to clear your mind, meditate, or listen to podcasts or music free of distractions. ■ During times of social distancing, it may be your only option. ■ There's no need to be embarrassed when you stop at Kroger for a sweaty bathroom break midrun.	■ There's less accountability, so it's easier to skip runs or not push yourself. ■ Long runs can get boring. ■ Running alone can be dangerous and scary at certain times and places. ■ There's no moral support in that final push of the marathon.
Running with a Friend or Training Buddy	■ You have someone to talk to and share your experience with. ■ There's plenty of time to spend with your bestie. ■ You've got accountability for those early morning runs. ■ You run faster when you want to impress someone.	■ Their pace might be slower or faster than yours. ■ You are spending a *lot* of time together. ■ For many reasons (e.g., scheduling, vacations, a pandemic), you may be running alone anyway. ■ You can't listen to your pump-up music.
Joining a Running Group	■ It's a great way to make new friends. ■ There are lots of options when it comes to people to talk to or speeds to run. ■ There's a wealth of experience to draw from for training and race day. ■ There are plenty of people cheering you on.	■ Training runs can be a bit hectic and aren't as relaxing. ■ You run on the group's schedule. ■ It's difficult to maintain social distancing. ■ No one else is stopping if you need to use the bathroom.

■ ■ ■ ■

Running along with Veteran Marathon Pacer *Jim Crist*

A pacer is hired by race organizers to help runners finish at their ideal times. There's a pacer for two-and-three-quarter-hour marathoners, and a pacer for five-hour marathoners, and a pacer for every increment in between. Each pacer runs a marathon at a predetermined rate—say 10-minute miles—which is marked on his or her bright bib. The pacer is the one calming you down at Mile 4, giving you a pep talk at Mile 18, and pushing you to your best at Mile 25.

Jim Crist has been pacing marathons for more than 20 years and has run in more than 100. Now he operates MarathonPacing.com, a company of runners who pace races around the country. His pacers are a cross between coaches, cheerleaders, and role models. The ideal pacer runs "evenly," Crist says. That means running at the same rate consistently, mile after mile. It's a rare ability. On average, his pacers have run about 30 marathons and have paced a dozen times. Here's what else he has to say about pacing.

How do you recommend using a pacer?

Often runners are intimidated or confused about joining a pace group. I explain to them that it should be just the opposite—that the groups are there to benefit the runners. Those runners who have no experience and are running their very first marathons should really seek out and join a pace group because they'll have a wealth of knowledge available to them as they go. There is a lot of stuff you can't read in a book, and a pacer can help you. Often, they have run the course before, and they know the ins and outs of such a grueling event.

What are your goals during the race as a pacer?

Certainly, you're paying attention to the time and your pace because you need to be very even, very accurate. But at the same time, you're talking to the people in your group. You're getting to know who they are and letting them know who you are so they have confidence in what you're leading them through. You're generally setting a positive tone for the event, which is important, because once you get to the later stages— say the last half-dozen miles—people are going to be low on energy. They might be chatty in the first 10 miles, but they're not chatty in the last six. At that point, you're the one doing all the talking, or maybe shifting from interactive conversation to just giving tips and observations and positive feedback.

What type of people are pacers?
All kinds. Some only pace one event a year. Others are ultramarathoners who ask to pace marathons on consecutive weekends because they're training for a longer race.

How do you decide at what pace the pacer should run?
It is slower than what they would run if they were racing. Loosely speaking, it is a minute a mile slower.

How long have marathoners been using pacers?
Thirty years ago, there really weren't pacers. The pros would use rabbits sometimes, but not pacers. A little more than 20 years ago, Clif Shot started a pace team, but it only paced a few of the big marathons. I started MarathonPacing.com around the same time, and using pacers has become more popular ever since. Now most marathons use pacers.

Famous Mile 2s

■ After crossing the Danube River, Mile 2 of the Vienna City Marathon in Vienna, Austria, takes runners past Prater, the city's famed amusement park. Towering above marathoners is the Wiener Riesenrad (German for Vienna Giant Wheel), which held the record for tallest Ferris wheel until 1985 and appeared in films like *The Third Man* and *Before Sunrise*.

■ While the Sydney Marathon in Australia's capital finishes at its famed opera house, runners can catch the best view of the theater during Mile 2. Coming across the Sydney Harbour Bridge, marathoners are treated to the picturesque image of the cresting opera house, set among the waves it was designed to resemble.

■ If you're looking for a challenge, try the Petra Desert Marathon, held every September, through the dusty hills of southern Jordan. While the race starts near the recognizable Al-Khazneh (seen in *Indiana Jones and the Last Crusade*), Mile 2 has runners wandering into the desert, where they'll remain for the entire final 25 miles. Bring extra water!

MILE 3

Aid Stations

It's Mile 3, and that means it's time for the race's first *aid station*! Look at all those beautiful volunteers. Their glistening, smiling faces. Their encouraging cheers. Their outstretched arms bearing waxy paper cups full of the correct proportion of Gatorade. These angelic humans, easily numbering into the thousands for many races, are out here to make sure you have your best race.

But aid stations are no laughing matter. Especially at major marathons, they are much more than a couple people and some water cups. They're full-blown operations. Those volunteers (hundreds per aid station) were up at the crack of dawn to set up thousands of cups full of water or sports drink. If the race starts at 7:00 a.m., they are completely set up well before then. When I volunteered at a New York City Marathon aid station, we started three hours before the runners arrived, and eight hours later, we were still raking up cups.

By the numbers, the 2019 New York City Marathon used 2.3 million cups at its aid stations, passing out 64,890 gallons of Poland Spring water, 110,000 Honey Stinger Energy Gels, and 14,000 Chiquita bananas.

Typically, marathons position aid stations every two miles or so. Aid station strategy? Elyse Kopecky says, "My dear friend Shalane [Flanagan] says, 'Drink soon and often.' It's better to drink constantly throughout the race. If you wait until you're thirsty, it's too late." For more information on how to tackle aid stations, see pages 42–43.

Drink water and thank all the superheroes out there with ponchos and sticky lemon-lime–scented hands.

<< New York City Marathon, New York, USA, 2013

Famous Mile 3s

■ If you're running a marathon in a state capital and you don't pass the capitol building, you've probably strayed off course at some point. The Denver Colfax Marathon leads its runners past the Colorado State Capitol in Mile 3. How does this differ from other capitol buildings you ask? Well, the dome is covered in gold leaf to commemorate the gold rush, the original event that led to thousands of people racing toward the Rocky Mountains.

■ As far as we know, King Arthur never ran a marathon, but those who take on the Edinburgh Marathon in Scotland will pass by the extinct volcano that bears his name. After passing the Palace of Holyroodhouse (the Queen's home in Scotland) during Mile 2, runners will encounter tourists' favorite hiking destination, Arthur's Seat, on their way out of town.

■ If you need a little spritzing during the big race to keep you cool, why not try the Victoria Falls Marathon? During Mile 3, you'll cross the Zambezi River in the face of the world's largest waterfall and its massive misting. If you're looking to run a race in every country (because who isn't?), this marathon will also help, as Mile 3 sees runners crossing from Zimbabwe to Zambia and back again.

 ## BODY CHECK—Water vs. Sports Drink

While we're here discussing the ins and outs of aid stations, let's break down the all-important choice of water or sports drink. Dr. George Chiampas, the medical director of the Chicago Marathon, says that "runners should determine their hydration plan well in advance of race day." My strategy of "just grab whatever and drink a lot," therefore, is not optimal. Based on your weight, your speed, how much you sweat, and how salty it is (do you have a lot of dried salt on your face at the end of a run?), you should calculate what you need to drink. Salty sweaters will need more sports drink.

He suggests weighing yourself before and after your long runs to determine how much fluid you need. You never want to lose more than two percent of your body weight, so if you're losing a higher percentage, then you need more fluids. If, however, you are gaining weight during a race, then you're definitely drinking too much. Plan ahead and practice your hydration plan during long runs. Oh, and the answer to the water or sports drink question is most likely both. ■

foot strike: the way the foot lands while running, typically classified as forefoot, midfoot, or heel

When tackling long distances, runners tend to fall into a rhythm, landing on the same part of their foot repeatedly. While most modern runners tend to land on their heels due to the cushioning in running shoes, historically forefoot strike—or landing on the ball of your foot—has been most prominent. Especially when running barefoot (or in old-timey Greek sandals), hitting the ground with the fatty front of your foot is more comfortable than the heel bone. Midfoot usually means you land on the heel and ball of the foot equally. Proper foot strike is a controversial topic in the marathon community, with experts fiercely debating which form is healthiest. Either way, knowing your foot strike is important so you can accommodate it and avoid injury. For example, if you've noticed pain in your heel and the rear of your running shoes are always worn down, you might want to consider buying shoes for people who strike with their heels. A good running store will be able to help you find the best ones. For more information, I also talk about pronation (another aspect of running that impacts your shoe choice) on page 58 and running shoes on page 60.

"I know I've got a rear foot strike because the heels of my Brooks are always worn down."

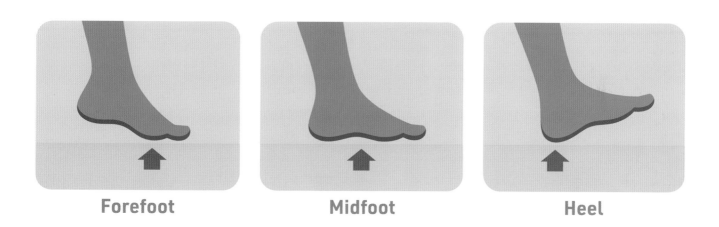

Forefoot   **Midfoot**   **Heel**

How to Tackle an Aid Station

Fill up that bottle. Want to skip all the tiny cups? Bring your own water bottle and ask aid station workers to fill it up. This can save you time in the long run. Run right up to the table (near the end of the line), and ask a pourer to fill up your bottle. It's not weird. They've been doing it all day.

Don't be the 12-cup person. Don't, however, try to fill up your water bottle with a dozen water cups. It's just not necessary, and you'll make a mess.

Is it water or Gatorade?
Most marathons offer both water and Gatorade at aid stations. They'll put the tables in the same order at each aid station, so if you're grabbing the second beverage, stay in the middle of the road as you run past the first.

Skip the station. If you're skipping the station, get in the middle and stay there.

Pour one out. Some cups are overflowing with liquid. Instead of drinking from a full cup, dump some water on the ground and drink out of an emptier cup. It's easier, I promise.

Ditch the cup. Once you've had your fill, toss your cup to the side of the road. Toss downward and look behind you before pitching so you don't nail a friendly runner in the face. And don't toss until you've cleared the station tables.

Grab from the back. Most runners grab cups from the first volunteers in line. Wait until the back of the line and you won't be fighting so many other runners.

Grab and go. Everyone is trying to grab fluids, so get out of the way. Once you grab your cup, head back to the middle of the road. Don't continue running next to the volunteers, blocking other runners.

Keep running. It can be tempting to slow down to savor your water, but resist the urge, at least at first. Slowing down can cause a bottleneck and create a dangerous situation as runners dodge their abruptly stopping counterparts. Grab the cup and get through the aid station before pulling up to the side of the road to walk and drink.

Squeeze that cup. Drinking while running is tricky. Pinch the brim of the cup closed to create a small hole, and then pour the water through the hole into your cheek. This prevents water sloshing on your face or choking you. Practice at home so you're a pro by race day.

43

"It's better to drink constantly throughout the race. If you wait until you're thirsty, it's too late."

Unusual Aid Station Foods

Sure, there are bananas, orange slices, and dozens of flavored gels, but that's not all that's being proffered along the marathon course. As marathons attempt to stand out from one another, many have started serving area-specific goodies along the course. The Vermont City Marathon, for example, hands out maple syrup shots—a nod to one of Vermont's key industries—midrun and then doles out Ben & Jerry's ice cream, another Vermont staple, at the finish. Baltimore, known for its cultlike love of Utz potato chips, has snack-size bags along the course for runners. In St. Louis, Crown Candy, a local candy shop, passes out chocolates. And those are just race-sanctioned treats.

It wouldn't be a marathon without random bystanders passing out an assortment of food and drinks, ranging from healthy (grapes, apple slices, saltines) to junk food (Pringles, Twizzlers, doughnut holes) to just plain bizarre (cheese dip, okra, jalapeños). And don't forget the "let's get this party started crew," enticing marathoners with a midrace beer or tequila shot. Always be careful about experimenting with foods midrun though. A vodka-cran at Mile 8 can really wreak havoc later on.

My personal favorite treat: ice pops. The Vermont City Marathon (truly a grade A event) passed out ice pops toward the end of the race. It was a godsend. Cold, refreshing, easy to suck down on the run, sugary. Any marathon not passing these out needs to reevaluate itself and *do better*!

Pages 44–45: New York City Marathon, New York, USA, 2013

MILE 4

Finding Your Rhythm

You've cleared your first aid station. The crowds have thinned a bit. Your body is warmed up. You are in this thing now. It's Mile 4, and it's time to find that groove you're going to sit in for As. Long. As. Possible. Sooner or later the wheels are going to fall off, but for now get into your rhythm. Whether you're using a pacer or a Garmin or just your natural intuition, find that happy place and keep on chugging along. Hopefully your body is so comfortable from running that this feels like nothing.

Most classic marathoners would be horrified at the thought of running 26.2 with music playing in their ears, but to them I say, "Who cares?" This is your marathon, and if music helps you find your rhythm and keeps you motivated then go for it. Personally, I love running with music, so I create playlists I know will keep me going. Some races don't allow headphones, though, so check that beforehand.

These next few miles should be pretty easy, so sit back and let your legs do their thing.

<< Copenhagen Marathon, Denmark, 2019

cadence: the speed at which a runner steps while running, usually measured in strides per minute

The two factors in determining your speed are cadence and stride length—how many strides you can take per minute, and how long each stride is. To determine your cadence, count the number of steps you take in a minute. Conventional wisdom is that 180 spm (strides per minute) is an ideal cadence, but your optimal cadence may vary quite a bit based on your height, weight, and running goals. A low cadence usually means a long stride length, which can lead to injuries and "braking" as your heel hits the ground far ahead of your body. A high cadence can mean you're spinning your legs a lot without covering much distance (i.e., going nowhere fast, but sweating a lot). An easy way to keep a consistent cadence is by running on the beat to music. There are plenty of playlists online with specific beats per minute for just this purpose.

"His cadence was 40 spm. Either he was going really slow, or he was doing the splits."

Famous Mile 4s

■ The Detroit Marathon is a prime example of exemplary diplomacy. During the race's fourth mile, runners cross the Ambassador Bridge and the Canadian border. A more-intense-than-usual sign-in process at the race expo involves a passport check, but it's well worth the hassle. Marathoners are treated to a sunrise as they cross the bridge to encouraging cheers from Border Patrol.

■ What's better than running by a beautiful ancient temple in Myanmar? How about running by dozens of beautiful ancient temples? Runners of the Bagan Temple Marathon, which rambles through the capital of the old Pagan Kingdom, will spy all kinds of treats in the world's largest archaeological site. At Mile 4, the tallest temple, Thatbyinnyu, rises above the course.

■ Technically every mile of the Antarctic Ice Marathon runs through the icy plains of the wintery continent, so Mile 4 isn't that noteworthy, but it is still in *Ant-freaking-arctica*! I think that's pretty cool. Also, as of 2020, the world's southernmost marathon costs $18,900 to run, so Mile 4 costs about $725. You might as well enjoy it!

✔ BODY CHECK – Private Parts

We're four whole miles in, so we're good to talk about some uncomfortable subjects, right? Running a marathon doesn't just affect your feet. It takes a toll on all body parts and that includes the ones that make your mom blush. So let's start with breasts (which to be fair I don't have), but they can swing more than five inches with each stride while running. Even for petite women, that's a *lot* of movement over 26.2 miles, and that can affect your running form and therefore lead to injuries. So a good bra is key. Moving on down, both men and women fall victim to sweaty nether regions, but for women that increases the risk of a yeast infection. In the name of good hygiene, both men and women should stick with sweat-wicking undergarments and clean up or shower postrun. Lastly, for the gents, picking underwear is important (so test it out on your training runs). Too tight and you can squeeze the testicles (ouch!), but too loose and they'll be bouncing around (also ouch!).

The horrors of chafing affect everyone no matter your unmentionables. With skin rubbing against other skin and your clothing for several hours, rashes and bleeding may occur where the sun doesn't shine. Experiment with different clothes to see what is the most comfortable long-term, and, in all circumstances, when in doubt, rub on some antichafing gel. For more on the wonderful world of chafing, see page 183. ■

For more on the wonderful world of chafing, see page 183.

roundup:
MUST-HAVE SONGS FOR A RUNNING PLAYLIST

Many runners find listening to music while running a cardinal sin, but if that's not you, here's some inspiration for your playlist.

Specific Songs

- "Turn the Page" by Bob Seger – *Des Linden*
- "Something Just Like This" by The Chainsmokers and Coldplay – *Danielle Quatrochi*
- "Take Me Home, Country Roads" by John Denver – *Dr. Mark Cucuzzella*
- "Countdown" by Beyoncé – *Matthew Huff*
- "Lose Yourself" by Eminem – *Meb Keflezighi*
- "U Gotta" by Orjan Nilsen and Fingerling – *Ryan Hall*
- "Nobody's Empire" by Belle and Sebastian – *Kate Carter*
- "Marathon" by Rush – *Michal Kapral*

Favorite Artists

- Taylor Swift – *Shalane Flanagan*
- AC/DC – *Greg McMillan*
- Drake – *Dr. George Chiampas*
- Neil Diamond – *Curt Munson*
- Fleetwood Mac – *Bennett Beach*
- Whitney Houston – *Kat Wang*
- The Beatles – *Lindsay Crouse*
- Kendrick Lamar – *Brinda Ayer*
- White Reaper – *Amanda McGrory*

Throughout my many interviews for this book, I asked my fabulous interviewees a set of rapid-fire questions to end our conversations. I've compiled their answers into roundups throughout the book.

■ ■ ■ ■
Running along with Running Club Leaders *Kat Wang and Brinda Ayer*

Plenty of people train, and run, their marathons alone. They don't have anyone who will run with them, it's more convenient, or they just need some me time. Many runners, however, find that running with others as part of a club can be an advantage. Two such individuals are Katharina "Kat" Wang and Brinda Ayer. Kat, who ran in college for New York University, is the coaching director of the New York Harriers, a running club that trains together in Central Park. Brinda didn't run much at all before she joined the North Brooklyn Runners (NBR) in 2016. Now she's the club's president. Here's why they love their running groups and think you shouldn't be afraid to join one yourself.

⌃ *Kat Wang*

What made you want to join a running club?

Kat: *I actually spent a year training for the Boston Marathon without a team, and one year was fine, but I didn't think I could do it again alone. It was awful having to go on your 20-mile training runs with nobody else. I met the Harriers for a great workout. I actually got injured shortly after that, and they still reached out to me because they noticed I was gone and wanted to make sure everything was OK. That was the moment I realized this was the team for me.*

Brinda: *I actually found NBR because they were offering a training run for the Brooklyn Half-Marathon. I just showed up. People were really warm and open, and there were so many young people my age. There were so many ability levels that it didn't feel intimidating. I went to another run a couple weeks later, and another after that, and then ran the Brooklyn Half wearing an NBR singlet. I was hooked.*

Can you tell me a little bit about your team?

Kat: *The Harriers have actually been around for more than 30 years at this point. The club was started by a group of guys. I think one of them was from the United Kingdom, hence the name "harrier." We have members ranging from people who just joined this year to people who joined at the club's inception in 1988. We have about 200 to*

250 total members. For active members, I'd say there are around 80 people at any given time. Our team varies in age and experience. I am always so appreciative of the running-team scene because most people only interact with their coworkers, so it's a really nice way to meet people who are doing all sorts of interesting things around New York City.

Brinda: *NBR is the largest free and volunteer-led club in New York. We have thousands of members. Our home base is in McCarren Park in Williamsburg, but we have offshoots in South Brooklyn/Prospect Park, Bushwick, and Central Brooklyn/Bed-Stuy. We're one big 1,700-person family.*

What types of things does the team do?

Kat: *We have weekly runs, which I plan around the New York Road Runners races, but our social scene is also strong. We do a lot of destination long runs. We do social events like running to doughnut shops or going to breweries on the weekend. It sort of kills two birds with one stone. You can be social, but also get your exercise out of the way.*

Brinda: *We offer up to 20 runs a week—sometimes two a day—which cater to everybody from very beginner runners who just need to get in two to three miles to sub-2:30 marathoners. In addition, since we're a big community organization, we participate in and volunteer for local races. You'll always find us manning a water table at the New York City Half-Marathon and Marathon. We also do fun social events. Every year we have this themed gala, which is basically a big party to celebrate all our achievements for the year, and we let loose, dress up, and have a little fun all together.*

What are the benefits of joining a running club?

Kat: *I think running with a team holds you more accountable because it's so easy, if you're running alone, to skip out on a run here and there. It's the encouragement to get out the door sometimes. You'll meet a lot of other*

BQ's MARATHON HISTORY
There's a Woman on the Course

Though there's evidence that a Greek woman named Melpomeni ran the very first Olympic Marathon route in 1896, women weren't officially allowed in the Olympic Marathon until 1984. Concerns ranged from sweaty impropriety to imminent danger of uterine collapse. But between 1896 and 1984, plenty of women went the distance. In 1966, Bobbi Gibb was the Boston Marathon's first (unsanctioned; fast) women's runner; she bandited the next two years as well. But Boston's first official female finisher was Syracuse University student Kathrine Switzer, who signed up for Boston in 1967 using her initials: K. V. Switzer. Wearing baggy sweats due to inclement weather, she was a few miles in before the race director, Jock Semple, realized she wasn't a he. Semple pounced, shouting at Switzer in a Scottish brogue, "Get the hell out of my race and give me those numbers!" Nearby news photographers caught multiple frames of the assault. Meanwhile, Switzer's football All-American boyfriend body checked Semple to the curb and Switzer outran them both to the finish.

people, who you might not have met in your daily life but who will enrich your life in general.

Brinda: *Showing up for somebody else is always more motivating than just keeping yourself accountable, not to mention it's more fun and you'll run faster. You have people you can pace with. Women in particular are running faster than they have before because of the pack mentality. You see all the elite runners do it. All the training groups in Kenya run together. That's a huge part of their strategy because it works. It psychologically works. It physiologically works. It's always easier to think about keeping up with somebody else than being in your own head about how tired you are.*

⌃ *Brinda Ayer*

What would you say to someone who has never run with other people and is nervous about holding others back or being embarrassed?

Brinda: *There's no such thing as holding anybody back. You have to run at the pace that's comfortable for you. The great thing about our group is that we have runners of all interests, goals, and experience levels. You will find someone in our group that will fit with you.*

"... find that happy place and keep on chugging along."

MILE 5

Gear and Equipment

If it takes a village to raise a child, it takes a closet full of running gear to run a marathon. Yes, technically you could run a marathon stark naked, drinking unfiltered water from the creek, but in today's age, 50 percent of marathon prep is buying cool stuff. But what is a necessity (Shalane Flanagan says, "Shoes are the gateway to your health"), and what is not (a $135 water bottle holster)?

The most important gear is what you're wearing because you'll be sweating in that ensemble for two to eight hours. Exactly what you're wearing doesn't matter that much as long as you've trained in it and you feel comfortable, so try out anything new on a long run before race day. I, for example, would not wear a cotton button-down for a marathon, but if you ran your 20-mile training run in that Express dress shirt and it felt good, then go for it. Shoes, socks, shorts, leggings, compression shorts, underwear, bra, shirt, running sleeves, hat, watch, sunglasses, hair tie—anything you're planning to wear on race day should be vetted. The same goes for your contingency plan outfits for bad weather. Practice running in your rain gear on a rainy day to troubleshoot any problems.

Next up there is the stuff going inside your body. Lots of people like to carry some gels (tiny packets of nutrient-rich goo you can squeeze into your mouth—think healthy ketchup packets!) or bring their own tiny water bottle. Others wear a hydration vest or carry some trail mix in a fanny pack. You do whatever is best for you, as long as it's tested and race approved. Don't decide that the marathon is the day to try out a CBD supplement your aunt said "did wonders for her," and if the race website says "no gallon water jugs," then don't bring yours to the course.

Last, men: tape your nipples.

<< *Chiang Mai Marathon, Thailand, 2018*

pronation: the way a foot rolls (inward or outward) as it makes contact with the ground to distribute the weight of impact

For a healthy runner, each foot should rotate around 15 percent inward with each stride, spreading the force of each foot strike across the entire foot. Typically, this means landing on the outside part of your heel and rolling your foot inward to push off with all toes evenly. Overpronation occurs when you rotate too far inward so the weight of propulsion is placed predominantly on the big toe. Supination is the opposite extreme, where you under rotate and spend most of your time on the outside of your foot. Both overpronation and supination can cause running-related injuries and can be treated with orthotics, strength training, stretching, and special shoes. Most running brands craft shoes specifically for various pronations, so if you know how your feet run, you can wear the ideal shoe.

"My pronation is a disaster. I overpronate and get all manner of hellish blisters on my big toe."

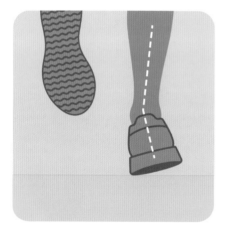

Overpronation

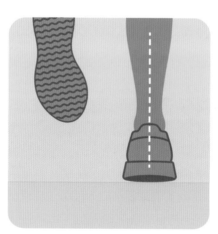

Neutral

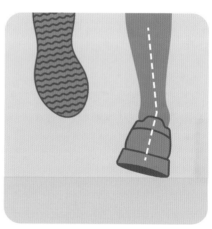

Supination

✔ BODY CHECK — Breathing

By Mile 5, your breathing should be at the level where it will remain for the majority of the marathon. If you're not breathing a little hard, you might want to push yourself a smidge. If you're sucking wind (as my grandma calls it), you're overexerting yourself. A common piece of advice is to run at a level where you can maintain a conversation but it's just a bit difficult. Dr. Mark Cucuzzella—a coach, professor, and top-tier runner with more than 100 marathons under his belt—dives deeper into the science of breath. "The key is abdominal breathing," he says. "A lot of people breathe with their chest and don't engage their diaphragm, so they overbreathe and hyperventilate." Quick, desperate breaths don't provide enough oxygen for your heart, brain, and muscles, which in turn increases stress and leads your body to more problems. Breathing deeply and rhythmically (try a four-count inhale through the nose and exhale through the mouth) not only oxygenates your entire body, but also syncs to your strides so your pace is more consistent. Good breathing equals good running. ■

roundup:
ONE PIECE OF GEAR YOU CAN'T LIVE WITHOUT

- Sketchers Go Run shoes – *Meb Keflezighi*
- My visor. I'm known for my collection of dirty, sweat-stained visors. – *Amby Burfoot*
- Nathan Hydration vest – *Elyse Kopecky*
- A hat. I can't stand hair in my face or the sun in my eyes. – *Bridget Quinn*
- Running vest – *Danielle Quatrochi*
- Oura Ring. It's the best sleep tracker, and it helps me balance my stress, sleep, and other patterns. – *Apolo Ohno*
- Good shoes – *Shalane Flanagan*
- Waterproof medical tape for the nipples – *Matthew Huff*
- Garmin watch – *Greg McMillan*
- Correct toes [silicone toe spacers that improve balance] – *Dr. Mark Cucuzzella*
- Brooks running shoes – *Des Linden*
- Merino wool shirt – *Curt Munson*
- Running shorts – *George Hirsch*
- Flip-up sunglasses for when it's shady and then sunny – *Dave Obelkevich*
- Asics running shoes. It's boring, but actually true. – *Ryan Hall*
- Adidas running shoes – *Bennett Beach*
- A buff. There is no end of uses! – *Kate Carter*
- Juggling balls – *Michal Kapral*
- My gloves. They're custom-made by a 3D printer. – *Amanda McGrory*
- Vaseline – *Kat Wang*
- Merino wool buff – *Brinda Ayer*

The Evolution of the Running Shoe

As long as people have been running they've had feet, and for much of the time, they've been wearing shoes.

490 BCE **Sandal or Barefoot**	Sadly, no photos from Ancient Greece exist, so we'll never know what the original marathoner shod his feet with, but it's a pretty good guess that it was either a thin-soled sandal or slipper or nothing at all.	
1832 **Rubber Soles**	While no marathons were being run at this time, Walt Webster did patent the process of adding rubber soles to canvas shoes, inventing the modern sneaker.	
1896 **Leather**	Near the turn of the century, the cool kids ran in leather shoes (with spikes, if you weren't on pavement).	
1920 **Dassler**	Adolf Dassler invented the modern running shoe with laces and everything. His company would eventually become Adidas.	
1951 **Onitsuka Tiger's** **Split-Toe**	Shigeki Tanaka won the Boston Marathon in a split-toe shoe inspired by traditional Japanese tabi socks, which have a pocket just for the big toe.	
1960 **New Balance Trackster**	The first mass-produced running shoe to feature both a ripple sole and a variety of widths, this shoe quickly became a favorite of cross-country teams and marathoners.	

Here is a brief history of the types of shoes marathoners have chosen to wear when running.

1972 **Nike Waffle Trainers**	The stuff of legend, Nike's Bill Bowerman poured rubber into his wife's waffle iron to create the first shoe with waffle soles for better traction.
1978 **Women's Shoes**	Men finally realized that women could also run and should have their own shoes. After Title IX's passing in 1972, brands began to launch women's lines over the next decade.
1994 **Brooks Adrenaline GTS**	A "go-to shoe" (get it?), this legendary road-running shoe came to market with plenty of cushioning, all the rage in the 1980s and 1990s.
2005 **Vibram FiveFingers**	A minimalist approach to running, these shoes mimicked bare feet and gave each toe its own little pocket, providing a back-to-basics running experience.
2009 **Hoka One One**	In contrast to minimalist shoes, Hoka's maximalist shoes provided runners with extreme amounts of cushioning to support their feet on all terrains.
2019 **Nike Vaporfly**	Eliud Kipchoge broke two hours wearing these foam-and-carbon shoes, but some claimed the shoe was so fast it was cheating.

Running along with Running Store Owner *Curt Munson*

While the original marathoner had very little in the way of gear aside from some sandals and an urgent message, today's runners rely on a plethora of supplies to keep them pounding the pavement. For marathoners hailing from Lansing, Michigan (like myself), the place to shop for shoes, gels, foam rollers, and body glide is Playmakers, a massive specialty store occupying an old Barnes & Noble. Longtime owner Curt Munson bought the tiny running store in 1981, growing the business over the subsequent decades. His knowledge on running products—and shoes in particular—is boundless. Here's what he had to share.

When choosing a shoe for marathon running, what are the key attributes you need to look for?

The shoe needs to have a good platform that sits underneath the foot properly. If you stand barefoot and then put your foot in the shoe, it should feel similar. Unfortunately, sometimes our industry gets caught up in a lot of fashion, and people come out with crazy shoes that aren't fundamentally functional.

What do you mean by a good platform?

When you look at a platform, you need a balanced, curved last so that it's shaped like your foot. [Last refers to the shape of the running shoe. A straight-last shoe is boxier, while a curved-last shoe is more crescent shaped.] In a shoe that's straight last, your foot pronates in more because it doesn't have the stability that it needs to have. Some companies said, "Gosh, people are landing on their heel. We should cushion that heel." In my mind, that was one of the biggest mistakes made because your foot has a tendency to roll more when you're rolling down the hill and then you don't engage your toes. Most shoes aren't shaped

Famous Mile 5s

■ While most marathons start in the wee hours of the morning, the Rock 'n' Roll Las Vegas Marathon doesn't fire its starting gun until the late afternoon, so you can run down the Vegas Strip in all its gawdy neon glory. Mile 5 leads runners past famed establishments like the Bellagio and Caesars Palace. Unfortunately, there are no penny slots on the course that I'm aware of.

■ There's no better place to spend January than Miami, Florida, on the beach. Turns out the Miami Marathon organizers had the same thought. Mile 5 of the marathon passes along South Beach (the one the diet was named after) before heading back into the heart of the city. It's the perfect cure for seasonal affective disorder.

■ If you're looking for a shady path, Irish accents, and the possibility of seeing a herd of wild fallow deer, then Mile 5 of the Dublin Marathon is the place for you. The fifth mile of Ireland's largest marathon turns runners onto a straightaway through Phoenix Park, Dublin's largest, which also happens to be known for its deer.

with the toes in mind. If you wear shoes that are pointed in the toe, after a while your whole foot is compromised. If the big toe has a good platform, though, it really helps stabilize the foot. Platform is the key base, but then you need materials that wrap your foot but don't infringe on it. Wrap the arch, have a little bit of heel support, and that's all you need.

Aside from shoes, what are the pieces of gear you think are most important?

Well, it's all secondary to the shoe, but it helps when you've got merino wool clothing. In the winter, your chances of staying out there and running are better. It's got the best temperature range, so it's good for hot and cold, and you don't have to pack as much. It also doesn't retain odor. I've worn merino wool pretty much every day for the last 15 years.

In addition to selling running products, you're also very involved in the Lansing community. What are some of your other endeavors?

Every weekend we've got races. We offer Good Form Running classes, which teach runners to run with their feet underneath them. It really has always been about being part of the community and giving back. That has been the key. The store has been recognized as a top store in the country, and that's because of the community.

MILE 6

The Runner's High

Mile 6 and you are *feeling good*! Whoever said marathoning was hard clearly didn't know what they were talking about. Almost an hour in and you're high-fiving the fans, flashing smiles at the aid station volunteers, and bopping along with the marching band that elected for some reason to serenade runners with *Wicked*'s "Defying Gravity."

This, my friends, is a fabled runner's high, which usually hits after a few miles of a long run and will last until the body inevitably starts to break down sometime after the halfway point. Runner's highs are caused by a mix of endorphins and endocannabinoids, which the body produces as a response to stress and physical discomfort. Basically, if your body is in some pain, but not that much, it starts to gush out chemicals to make you feel euphoric. That's why runners often feel better in Mile 10 than Mile 2.

Be forewarned, though, the runner's high is an evil temptress, especially when combined with the cheering crowds. It can easily push you to go out too quickly, which will bite you in the butt later when the magic chemicals have been depleted. Enjoy the high, but stick to your pace. There's no need to crash any sooner than you have to.

<< *Athens Marathon, Greece, 2019* **Pages 64–65:** *San Francisco Marathon, California, USA, 2016*

> **"The runner's high is an evil temptress . . . it can easily push you to go out too quickly."**

Famous Mile 6s

■ The Walt Disney World Marathon sprinkles no shortage of magic on runners. In addition to fireworks at the start, photo ops with Mickey and Minnie along the course, and the possibility of riding rides during the race (yes, you read that right), the marathon winds through all four parks. Mile 6 takes place almost entirely in the Magic Kingdom, meaning awestruck runners cruise down Main Street toward Cinderella Castle, their jaws dragging along on the ground and pixie dust in their hair.

■ An equally stacked Mile 6 runs along the North Shore of Pittsburgh in its yearly marathon. Not only does it pass PNC Park (home of the Pirates), Heinz Field (home of the Steelers), and the Carnegie Science Center, but most of the mile runs along Pittsburgh's famed rivers. Watch the Monongahela and Allegheny form the Ohio in the City of Bridges.

■ As an early Christmas gift to yourself, why not run 26.2 in Hawaii? The Honolulu Marathon, running every December, is one of the largest in the United States. With no qualifying times, time limit, or cap on the number of runners allowed, it is a favorite of beginners. Mile 6 passes the famed Waikiki Beach, but don't worry, no on-sand running is required.

long slow distance: lengthy training runs used to increase mileage and run somewhat slower than race pace

Typical marathon training plans revolve around long weekend runs leading up to race day. For many nonprofessional runners, these are long slow distance (LSD) runs, which are run at a moderate intensity during which you can have a conversation while running. LSD helps your body acclimate to the wear and tear you may feel on race day, so that when you're entering the back half of the marathon your body is used to the microinjuries that running a long distance creates. LSD also contributes to good heart and lung health (which everyone will comment on if you ever donate blood). Wins all around!

"Sorry I'm late to brunch. I was just pounding out a 20-mile LSD. Please hold your applause, and add a side of bacon."

✔ BODY CHECK—Sweat

By Mile 6, you should have worked up a sweat (unless you're one of those crazy shirtless men prowling the starting line in 30-degree weather). Some things to know:

1. People sweat different amounts, so if you're drenched on a five-miler you better be drinking more water.

2. Some people's sweat is saltier than others, so if you've got a lot of white dust caked on your face at the end of a long run, you need to take in some salt during the race.

3. Hyperhidrosis is a condition where you sweat a lot, either all over or in one place, and a doctor might be able to help you out with this.

4. Sweat-wicking clothes are your friend. Sweaty cloth rubbing on skin can cause chafing (bad), sweaty feet can cause warts (also bad), and sweaty areas can get infected (really bad). Evaporation is our friend. ■

Running along with Marathon Coach *Greg McMillan*

Many marathoners (including yours truly) tackle their first 26.2 with a hodgepodge of advice culled from friends, the internet, and their own intuition. Serious runners, however, often turn to a marathon coach to craft workout plans built specifically with their goals, schedule, and ability in mind. One such coach is Greg McMillan.

Greg is a national champion runner, holds a master's degree in exercise physiology focused on distance running, and has written multiple books on the sport. He is also a USA Track and Field (USATF)-certified coach who has trained everyone from Olympians to your uncle Saul, who has taken up running again after his divorce. One of the most common marathoning milestones is qualifying for Boston, an extremely difficult task for the average runner, and Greg has coached more than 10,000 Boston qualifiers! Needless to say, the man knows a thing or two about marathons, so I spent some time picking his brain. His pearls of wisdom are strewn throughout the pages of this book, but start here.

What made you want to become a running coach?

If you study exercise science in college like I did, people start asking you for advice and you tell them what you've been learning or what you've experienced as a runner yourself, and then you give them a workout, and then you give them a training plan, and then suddenly they call you "coach." I didn't go into it thinking I'd be a running coach. I was just passionate about this sport myself and happy to share what I learned with other people.

What do you do on a daily basis as a running coach?

Mostly, you're trying to educate the runner to coach themselves, so they can make run-day decisions about what they should do. I plan the training, get the feedback on the training, and then make any adjustments. The biggest challenge is making all that fit into busy life schedules. We know what we want to do, but doing it within regular life is the challenge.

So what's the solution? Just waking up earlier?

The main strategy is efficiency, so you're looking for what training will give you the biggest bang for your buck when you have limited time. Or you can capitalize on scheduling by pushing the higher-stress training days to the lowest life-stress days.

What training must-dos have you found people commonly neglect?

In training in general, people try to avoid suffering. They don't like to feel uncomfortable, so they try to set up their training to ignore suffering. They'll make sure they have all their fueling and are never tired and never pushed to the point where it gets really challenging. The race itself does involve a lot of suffering. A lot of runners mess up training because they don't challenge themselves with enough suffering.

Any other tips?

You have to learn a fueling strategy [what you're going to eat and drink both during the race and in the days leading up to it] that can better help you. If athletes aren't working on race-type fueling, then they get in the race and their body may not react well.

▼ ▼ ▼

BQ's MARATHON HISTORY
Victory for ~~Japan~~ Korea

At the 1936 Berlin Olympics, Sohn Kee-chung became the first Asian Olympic Marathon winner, a nice poke in the racist eye of Nazi Germany. Sohn was also the first Korean athlete to win an Olympic medal, though that wasn't obvious to the world at large. With their country occupied by Japan since 1910, Sohn and his teammate, bronze medalist Nam Sung-yong, had to compete under the auspices of Japan. That included racing under a Japanese version of his name, Son Kitei, along with the Japanese flag and national anthem at his awards ceremony. While the Japanese anthem played, Sohn and Nam both bowed their heads in what they later called "silent shame and outrage," while Sohn covered the Japanese flag on his uniform. Korean newspapers also blurred out the Japanese flag in photographs of the event, resulting in being shut down, their journalists arrested and even tortured. After liberation, Sohn spent the rest of his life in South Korea, where he coached two Boston Marathon winners and an Olympic gold medalist.

MILE 7 Nutrition

Lucky number seven. Congratulations, you're nearing the one-hour mark! While your body is hopefully still chugging along on cruise control, let's have a quick chat about nutrition.

Especially for the young and uninitiated, running a marathon is seemingly most dependent on general athletic fitness and proper training. All your body parts work? You did some training runs? Congrats! You're good to go. Except, maybe not. The no-stretching, little-sleep, all-I-eat-is-Arby's mentality may be fine for lesser events, but the marathon is *very different* than a basketball game or swim meet. In order to last seven miles, let alone 26.2, you need proper fueling. What begins as fatigue or a sloshy stomach at Mile 7 can be a full-blown DNF (did not finish) by Mile 22 if you're not careful.

Beyond just finishing the race, good nutrition is important for your health throughout the entire marathon process. Training takes a lot out of you, especially in those weeks where you're racking up 40-plus miles, and not eating good carbs, proteins, and fats can leave you depleted, susceptible to sickness, and with sloppy form (the gateway drug to a leg injury).

I've said it before, and I will say it again: *drink water*! Hydration is key to all aspects of life. We are, after all, 60 percent water.

<< Athens Marathon, Greece, 2015

carb-loading: the act of eating a large amount of carbohydrates before a marathon to stockpile fuel for the race

While exercising, your body transforms food into the energy it needs to press on. Carbs, which your body converts to glycogen, are a particularly good source of fuel. During an endurance event like the marathon, your body will need as much fuel as possible, so runners employ the carb-loading strategy of eating more carbs than usual in the week before a race in order to stash extra glycogen. Avoid cramming extra carbs the night before to prevent big chunks of undigested food in your system. Instead, eat carbs regularly in the days before and then top off your supply with 150 grams of carbs three hours before your race.

"Who wants to go to Olive Garden? I've got to carb-load for my marathon this weekend."

 ## BODY CHECK — Eating during the Race

I don't know about you, but I get hungry between meals on a normal day when I'm just replying to emails. So it makes sense that our bodies need additional nutrients in the three to six hours of running a marathon (not to mention the hour or so you shouldn't eat before the start!). How do you get those calories into your body while running 26.2? Elyse Kopecky has some tips:

1. Sports drinks are your friend. While she wouldn't recommend sipping a Gatorade casually at home, Elyse says, "when you're running crazy mileage, a sports drink can really save your butt. It's great to have something that replaces all the lost electrolytes, but also has the simple sugars that your body can process and use immediately for energy."

2. Try nut butter. Especially if you have a high metabolism or are going to take longer than four hours on the course, you probably need something more substantial than Powerade. "I love nut butter goos," says Elyse. "They have dates and cashews, and it's a nut butter, so it's good fat." Sometimes she makes her own versions at home, but she also loves the Muir Energy brand.

3. Be wary of bold claims. "There are all these foods that sound amazing and have all these bold health claims that are marketed to runners and will promise a lot, but most of those foods are pretty void of nutrition and hard to digest," says Elyse. Test everything on training runs to see how your body reacts, and try making your own race-day pick-me-ups with natural ingredients. ■

Famous Mile 7s

■ While bridges are pretty to look at, they can be nightmarish in a marathon, mostly because a bridge is just a man-made metal hill. Mile 7 of the Hong Kong Marathon brings with it the mile-long Stonecutters Bridge that stretches over the Rambler Channel at a maximum height of nearly 1,000 feet. Add the typically high level of humidity to the equation, and you've got a potentially potent marathon. But hey! The view of Hong Kong is stunning!

■ Speaking of bridges, the San Francisco Marathon has also planted a well-known bridge at its seventh mile. Runners of this equally hilly marathon run back and forth across the Golden Gate Bridge before completing their loop of the city. If it's not too foggy, bridge crossers can spy the infamous Alcatraz prison to the east in San Francisco Bay.

■ Although the Lisbon Marathon is named after Portugal's capital city, it actually spends most of its time elsewhere. The first seven miles of the course zip back and forth along the beaches of Cascais on the Atlantic Ocean. Let the sea breeze cool you off on this flat course before heading to the finish in downtown Lisboa.

■ For runners looking to complete a marathon in every state (or just looking for an excuse to visit Alaska), the Anchorage Mayor's Marathon, run every June, is a tantalizing option. Miles 7 through 17 wind through the beautiful Chugach State Park, known for its scenic mountains, forests, glaciers, and some of the best marathon air quality around.

"... in order to last seven miles, let alone 26.2, you need proper fueling."

■ ■ ■ ■

Running along with Marathon Nutrition Guru *Elyse Kopecky*

If you're looking for information on how food affects marathon runners' bodies, there's hardly a better person to chat with than Elyse Kopecky. A chef and nutrition coach, but also a runner herself, Elyse certainly knows the topic well. So well, in fact, that she and her college bestie from the University of North Carolina cross-country team, Shalane Flanagan, wrote two cookbooks specifically for runners. Both *Run Fast. Eat Slow.* books found their way onto the *New York Times* best-seller list, and the recipes and tips they shared spurred Shalane to win the New York City Marathon. Luckily, Elyse agreed to share some tasty nutrition tidbits with us.

What is the difference between a typical healthy diet and a healthy diet for marathon runners?

A marathoner needs an incredible amount of nourishment. You can get by with a bad diet when you're just running three to four miles a couple days a week, but when you move up in distance, your body will completely break down if you aren't eating right. Runners really need to embrace spending equal amounts of time running and working in the kitchen to cook nourishing meals that are a good balance of carbs, proteins, and fats. Runners also need a lot more minerals than most people because the body depletes minerals a lot faster when you're running a lot of miles. It's really good to work with a doctor to have your nutrient levels measured to see if you have any deficiencies.

What types of minerals do runners usually run low on?

Iron for women. I recommend eating a lot of iron-rich foods like grass-fed beef, leafy greens, and dark chocolate. I also use a lot of blackstrap molasses in my baking. Runners also need a lot of magnesium, calcium, and vitamin D. You can get a lot of good minerals from nuts and seeds, but it's about finding the right balance for your body. Eating too many nuts can be hard on digestion. If you're running a lot of miles, your blood is flowing away from your digestive system to your hardworking muscles, so your digestion might be more sensitive.

GO-TO RACE-DAY BREAKFAST

- A bagel and a banana – *Amanda McGrory*
- Egg sandwich – *Danielle Quatrochi*
- Race-day oatmeal (from my cookbook, *Run Fast. Eat Slow.*) – *Shalane Flanagan*
- An egg sandwich three hours before the start – *Greg McMillan*
- Pop-Tarts, either strawberry or blueberry frosted – *Kat Wang*
- A bagel with peanut butter, white rice, and coffee – *Des Linden*
- Eggs and himbasha bread that my mom makes – *Meb Keflezighi*
- A cup of coffee and a white bagel – *Amby Burfoot*
- Oatmeal, nuts, or yogurt, and a hard-boiled egg with lots of salt – *Bridget Quinn*
- A banana and half a bagel – *Dave Obelkevich*
- Maltodextrin powder with Muscle Milk protein powder – *Ryan Hall*
- Cereal—I'm in a cereal club, and I like to mix five different kinds at once – *Bennett Beach*
- A toasted bagel with peanut butter and a cup of tea – *Kate Carter*
- An everything bagel – *Matthew Huff*
- Oatmeal and a banana – *Michal Kapral*
- Superhero muffins – *Elyse Kopecky*
- Whatever I can find as I'm frantically throwing things in my bag for the race – *Lindsay Crouse*
- A carb with peanut butter and maybe a few dates – *Brinda Ayer*

Are there foods that runners shouldn't be eating?

You can have too much of a good thing. Runners tend to overdo it. We are very much type A, and we think, "Oh, kale is really good for me. I'm going to eat kale at every meal." Then we have digestive distress from eating too much. A lot of cruciferous vegetables can be really hard to digest, such as broccoli, cauliflower, and Brussels sprouts, or eating too many legumes or beans or too much dairy or gluten. Everyone's digestion is different. It's really important to figure out what works best for you.

What should runners be eating in the lead-up to the marathon?

Runners tend to want to carb-load the day before the race, but it can be too much. It's more important to add more complex-carb snacks throughout the entire week leading up to the marathon to top off your glycogen stores—not just the day before. I like easier-to-digest complex carbs like sweet potatoes, rice, or oatmeal versus having a big bowl of pasta that can leave you feeling bloated. My favorite dinner the night before a race is a power bowl with rice, chicken, or salmon, roasted sweet potatoes, and avocado.

What about the morning of?

What's most important is to eat exactly what you do while training that works best for your long runs. It's tempting to try all the samples from the race expo, but it's important to eat what's best for you. My go-to is a superhero muffin [the recipe is in her cookbook]. A big

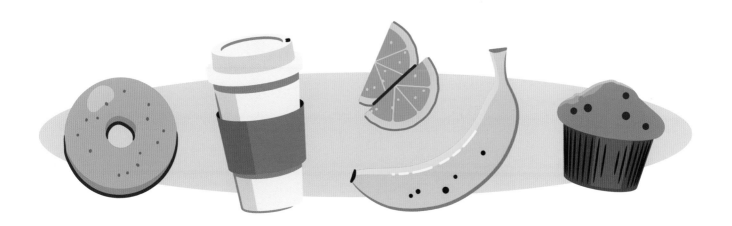

bowl of oatmeal is Shalane's go-to. I find straight oatmeal to be a little too heavy for me. And always drink before long runs. I drink lemon gingerade. I make it with fresh lemon juice, ginger, and some sea salt. It's hydrating and soothing for digestion.

Any other pro tips?

People can be so regimented with their running and so strict and hard on themselves. It's important to listen to your body, and there can be times in our lives when running is not serving us well. If you take a year off to reset or start a new career or have a baby, that's OK. Running will always be there for you to come back to. It's good to take time off because you'll come back appreciating all running has to give.

MILE 8 Terrain

As with life, the marathon has its uphills and downhills. By Mile 8, you've probably faced a little of each. Moreover, some marathons are significantly harder than others. Much of that depends on the course's terrain.

When training for a marathon, keeping the course's elevation in mind is important; for example, if you're showing up to the Pikes Peak Marathon without having practiced running some hills, you're in danger. Most races have elevation charts online, so you can scope out what your marathon's terrain looks like. Pro tip: Take a close look at the graph's scale because, depending on that, a flat course can look hilly or a mountain range can appear unintimidating.

Once you're on the course, run with the terrain in mind. If you're in Boston and you know that the dreaded Heartbreak Hill is coming in the back half, you're going to want to save more energy than if you're running in Chicago, which is pancake flat. Knowing when to conserve and when to push is key in a four-hour event.

And always keep in mind that with every uphill comes the downhill, so while you're slaving away, look forward to that sweet, sweet descent to come.

<< Jungfrau Marathon, Switzerland, 2011

Famous Mile 8s

■ Plenty of praying goes on during the marathon, so it only makes sense that marathon courses often pass churches. Few, however, are grander than the Basílica de la Sagrada Família, which sits along the course in Mile 8 of the Barcelona Marathon. The basilica, which began construction in 1882, is still unfinished due to conflicts in the area and incredibly ambitious designs. The current goal for completion is 2026. See, there are things that take longer than a marathon!

■ Austin, Texas, proclaims itself "weird" and wants to keep it that way. The Austin Marathon weaves itself through plenty of the city's quirky neighborhoods on its way to the capitol building at the finish. Mile 8 cruises along the Colorado River as it winds through the city known for barbecue, live music, tacos, and bats.

■ Few hotels are as instantly recognizable as the Burj Al Arab, the sail-shaped mammoth off the coast of Dubai. While Dubai's marathon doesn't make its way out to the man-made island on which the hotel sits, it does pass the 56-floor structure multiple times, including in Mile 8. In the marathon's loop-shaped course, the hotel serves as an iconic reference point as marathoners circle the United Arab Emirates' largest city.

✔ BODY CHECK — The Feet

Some of the most heated debates in the marathon community revolve around shoes. The two predominant theories:

1. Buy a shoe with a big, fat cushion because you're pounding on the pavement and you need a shock absorber.

2. Buy a minimal shoe (if you wear shoes at all) because cushions weaken the leg muscles and cause more injuries over time.

No matter your shoe, however, strengthening your foot is advantageous. Dr. Mark Cucuzzella describes the foot as "basically a spring," saying, "think of your foot like a superball, but after it fatigues it becomes more like a Hacky Sack [i.e., a lot less springy]. That's the purpose of training: to have a stronger and more resilient foot, so that at a mile when most people are thudding the ground, you can still feel springy."

Another pro tip is to buy shoes that give your big toe some space. "So many people squeeze into shoes that have really narrow toe boxes, so it puts the big toe out of its natural position," he says. Moving your big toe changes your stride, which can hurt your knees, your back, your neck, and your performance overall. Moral of the story: treat those feet good. Train them and buy shoes that really fit.
For more information on running shoes, see pages 60–61. ■

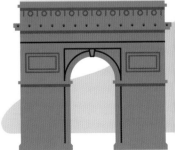

runcation: a vacation planned specifically around running, either a race or recreationally

With marathons run in all 50 states and on seven continents, many races require travel, so why not plan a vacation around your 26.2? Pick a city you've always wanted to visit, sign up for its marathon, and then schedule sightseeing around the race! For nearby destinations, a long weekend runcation may be a nice chance to explore. Travel abroad for an extended running vacay. Helpful hint: schedule your marathon for the middle of your trip, so you aren't running jetlagged or wiped out from intense sightseeing. An alternative is incorporating runs into a preplanned vacation. There's no better way to explore a new city, and trail runs are a nice way to unwind and reconnect with nature.

"I won the Tokyo lottery so now I've got a Japanese runcation to plan!"

BQ's MARATHON HISTORY
A Marathon Comeback

One of 13 children from a remote village in Veracruz, Mexico, Germán Silva pursued running despite his father's disapproval. When pressured into something sensible, like working in the family's orange grove, Silva ran the other way. All the way to the 25th running of the New York City Marathon, when, at the age of 26, Silva and his countryman Benjamín Paredes broke from the men's lead pack with three miles to go. The training partners ran neck and neck in the 1994 race until Mile 25.5—just seven-tenths of a mile from the finish—when Silva veered prematurely into Central Park, following the race director's vehicle, while Paredes stayed on course. After a dozen strides, "Wrong Way Silva" realized his mistake, reversed course, and turned on a blistering kick. He won in 2:11:21, just two seconds ahead of Paredes. Silva's brilliant recovery was the perfect gift for his now-proud father, who celebrated his 70th birthday the following day.

Elevation Charts

Is it a fast course? Does it having rolling hills? Let's do some elevation chart comparisons to see just how these marathon courses differ.

■ **Twin Cities Marathon (Minneapolis and St. Paul, Minnesota):** This is a standard marathon course. There are some uphills and downhills, but with only a 200-foot elevation change, most of them are slight.

■ **Baltimore Marathon (Baltimore, Maryland):** A slightly harder version of standard, Baltimore includes two major hills, but again the elevation changes are only a few hundred feet spread over miles, so nothing drastic.

▨ **Boston Marathon (Boston, Massachusetts):** Boston is generally considered a difficult course despite being downhill overall. Why? Because the back half is significantly hillier, and by then your legs are tired. A mountain in Mile 6 is easier than a bump in Mile 20.

■ **Berlin Marathon (Berlin, Germany):** If you're looking for an easy, injury-free run, and possibly a PR (personal record), you want flat! Berlin provides that. It barely changes 100 feet in the whole course.

▨ **California International Marathon (Sacramento, California):** This marathon attracts a lot of runners each year hunting for a PR because it is a downhill race, meaning you've got momentum on your side nearly the entire time.

■ **Hatfield-McCoy Marathon (South Williamson, Kentucky):** Racing isn't just about time. Sometimes you want a challenge. With more than 600 feet of elevation incline and decline in the front half, followed by constant rolling hills in the back, this is a workout.

▨ **Whiskey Row Marathon (Prescott, Arizona):** Run up and down the same mountain *twice*. This race has you storming more than 1,000 feet two times, each followed by a swift descent, which can be rough on the knees.

■ **Jungfrau Marathon (Interlaken, Switzerland):** If you're looking for a real killer, why not do an uphill-only race with a 6,500-foot elevation change? Basically, you're just hiking an Alp for 26.2 miles.

■ **World's Fastest Marathon (Granada, Spain):** And then there's the opposite. If you want a crazy PR, try this aptly named 6,000-foot downhill marathon out of Spain's Sierra Nevada mountain range. Your knees may not thank you though.

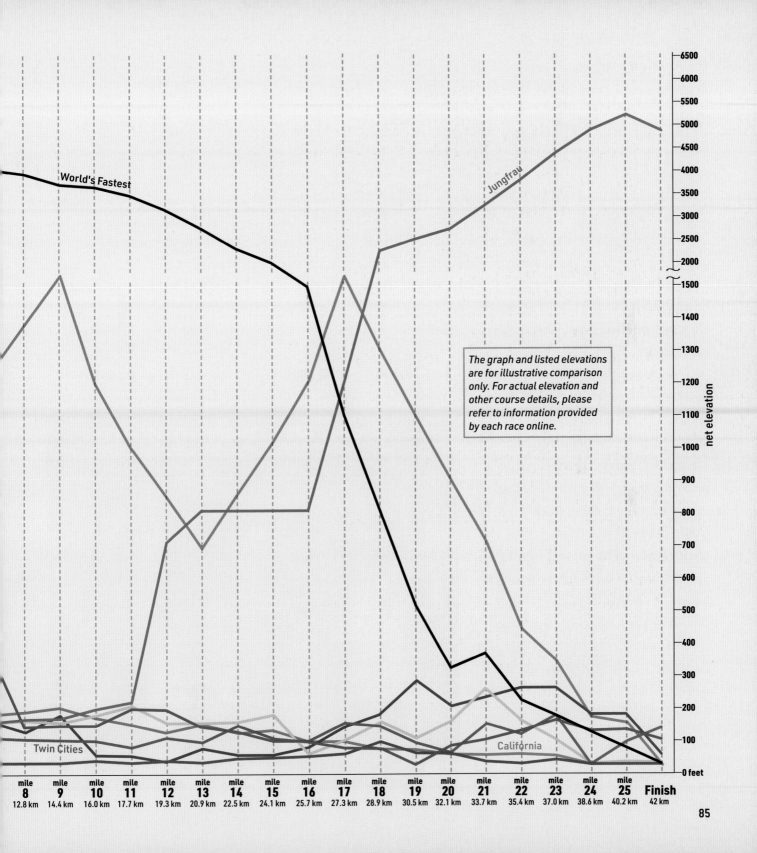

World's Fastest

Jungfrau

The graph and listed elevations
are for illustrative comparison
only. For actual elevation and
other course details, please
refer to information provided
by each race online.

net elevation

Twin Cities

California

mile 8	mile 9	mile 10	mile 11	mile 12	mile 13	mile 14	mile 15	mile 16	mile 17	mile 18	mile 19	mile 20	mile 21	mile 22	mile 23	mile 24	mile 25	Finish	
12.8 km	14.4 km	16.0 km	17.7 km	19.3 km	20.9 km	22.5 km	24.1 km	25.7 km	27.3 km	28.9 km	30.5 km	32.1 km	33.7 km	35.4 km	37.0 km	38.6 km	40.2 km	42 km	

6500
6000
5500
5000
4500
4000
3500
3000
2500
2000
1500
1400
1300
1200
1100
1000
900
800
700
600
500
400
300
200
100
0 feet

▪ ▪ ▪ ▪
Running along with Race Operator *Joe Connelly*

When you run a marathon, you're essentially worrying and preparing for yourself. When you *plan* a marathon, you're prepping and worrying on behalf of the thousands of runners who will be attempting to survive the experience you devise for them. You are responsible for a seamless process that requires volunteers and street blockages and swag and extends from registration through the finish-line tape.

Joe Connelly is the director of race operations for RunVermont, the organization that oversees the Vermont City Marathon, the state's largest. The race spans the entire city of Burlington and boasts more than 6,000 participants, 1,700 volunteers, 170 course monitors, and approximately 50 cops.

Joe and his team began planning for the May 2018 race in 2017, thinking 15 months ahead on tweaks and changes based on the 2016 running. Any new ideas—like a left turn on Church Street instead of a right, or tape stations for battered feet—are planned out and then tested on a small scale in the 2017 race. If they work, they are added for everyone the following year.

According to Joe, a good course makes intuitive sense, provides visual stimuli ("Look, Ma, it's Lake Champlain!"), and produces fast times. That's harder to achieve than you might think. In fact, the moment a race is over, Joe and his team are analyzing what worked and what didn't, from beginning to end. During this eight-week postmortem, he scrutinizes runner surveys, interrogates his volunteers, and interviews city officials to figure out how to do it better.

When he's not trying to plan for the free radicals that could affect his marathon (flooding, heat waves, fires, gas leaks, bomb threats), he's focusing on the minutiae he can control.

What is your strategy for aid stations?

We put one about every mile and a half until the 20-mile mark, and then we go every mile. That gives our medical personnel a chance to watch runners more frequently at the end.

How do you handle security?

It has ramped up in the last five years. We have a monthly meeting at the police station. We have about 55 cops who do traffic duty, and that's a lot more than just Burlington police; we have cops from every district around.

What does a successful marathon look like?

Success is everybody goes home [alive].

IDEAL RUNNING VACATION DESTINATIONS

- Switzerland Valleys – *Shalane Flanagan*
- Greece – *Dr. George Chiampas*
- The Alps – *Dr. Mark Cucuzzella*
- Anywhere near water or mountains – *Apolo Ohno*
- Chamonix, France – *Des Linden*
- Mackinac Island, Michigan—no cars and lots of hills and trails – *Curt Munson*
- Mission Bay in San Diego, California – *Meb Keflezighi*
- Upper Peninsula of Michigan – *Matthew Huff*
- Places with trails, like Northern Italy or Sun Valley, Idaho – *George Hirsch*
- New Mexico – *Dave Obelkevich*
- Ethiopia and Kenya—the mecca of running – *Ryan Hall*
- London—because I haven't run the marathon yet – *Danielle Quatrochi*
- Bhutan Marathon—it's on my bucket list – *Kate Carter*
- The French Alps or Bend, Oregon – *Elyse Kopecky*
- The Maldives – *Michal Kapral*
- The Catskills – *Kat Wang*
- Uzbekistan—dry heat and open roads – *Lindsay Crouse*

MILE 9

Bathrooming

The body can revolt in many ways over the course of the marathon. None is more annoying than "the urge" setting in, especially during a race. But to quote *Jurassic Park*, "When you gotta go, you gotta go." The goal then is to avoid, you know, pooping.

I debased myself and asked some of the pros about their strategies. "Become a fan of coffee," Des Linden told me. "It just makes things much easier, and it's delicious. My husband and I have a coffee company, and we roast our own beans. It's called Linden by Two, and we carry it on the road."

Shalane Flanagan added, "Everyone has to factor in their circadian rhythm. I'll start to adjust going to bed earlier or waking up earlier to get my system on the time zone change." With races around the world, this can definitely be a factor.

Here's the thing: races do a great job of having port-o-johns all over the place because they don't want runners defecating on people's lawns. Worst-case scenario, you can use one of those. But my strategy (and it has worked every time so far, knock on wood) is to drink a lot of coffee on the day before the race. Clean out the system the night before, and then go again before the race. Hopefully that will leave you feeling light and breezy.

<< Boston Marathon, Massachusetts, USA, 2018

Famous Mile 9s

- The Wright Brothers flew so that we could run . . . where they flew . . . after they ran. It's slightly complicated, but marathoners who embark on the Outer Banks Marathon in Kitty Hawk, North Carolina, will find themselves passing the birthplace of flight and the Wright Brothers National Memorial at Mile 9. Honor Wilbur and Orville Wright by pounding out the remaining 17.2 and flying home.

- To the chagrin of many runners or tourists, there is still no Hobbiton Marathon, so those looking to run in New Zealand must make do with the spectacularly beautiful Wellington Marathon. The race runs almost entirely along the coast of the island nation, venturing out to Point Halswell and its photogenic, checkered lighthouse at Mile 9.

- Oh look, the Detroit Marathon is back again. (It's almost as if I'm from Michigan and Detroit was my first marathon!) Mile 9 of this exquisitely crafted race sees runners emerging from the Detroit-Windsor Tunnel as they return from Canada. Marathoners erupt from a mile-long tunnel into the historic downtown, the iconic five-towered Renaissance Center presiding majestically over the skyline. I'm getting goosebumps just thinking about it.

MARATHON VOCAB WORD

roadsiding: the act of using the bathroom in an emergency midrun, either by finding a restroom or "going" in the wild

Running jostles your digestive system and causes blood to flee your GI tract, often creating a need for runners to go number two. Marathons provide plenty of methodically placed port-o-johns, but 20-mile training runs may leave you in a lurch. Search your routes prerun for restaurants, parks, or convenience stores you can use in case of an emergency. If desperate in a residential area, there is no shame in knocking on a stranger's door. It's better to beg someone you'll never see again than poop on the sidewalk. Rural runners might want to stick a few sheets of toilet paper in their pockets for emergencies.

"I've never been happier to see a construction site port-o-john. I was terrified I'd roadside in my pants."

☑ BODY CHECK — Pooping

We all know how to poop (hopefully). The key to marathoning is not pooping for 26.2 miles. Elyse Kopecky says, "The reason runners end up in port-o-johns is because of nerves. Your body just wants to eliminate." The solution is trying to use that nervous energy to your advantage. "It's good to be nervous the morning of the race to let your body eliminate before you get to the race course." Elyse's writing partner, Shalane Flanagan, adds, "The key for me is coffee, and getting up early." Coffee is a marathoner favorite for stimulating the bowels, but the issue is timing. Drink the coffee too late, and the urge can strike an hour or so in (say Mile 9?). Get up early, use the ol' stress-and-coffee combo to purge the system, and then head to the starting line. And, as with anything, you should do plenty of training runs for trial and error with no official times or people fighting you for a gas station bathroom. ▪

"Everyone has to factor in their circadian rhythm . . . start to adjust going to bed earlier or waking up earlier to get [your] system on the time zone change."

Marathon Etiquette

Marathons, just like weddings, basketball games, or tea parties, have etiquette. Here are some basic dos and don'ts to save you from humiliation and make your 26.2 smooth.

☐ **Steer clear of wheelchairs.** While wheelchair racers start before the runners, if you're in an early corral you may pass one or two on an uphill. Be aware on the downhill, though, because they can coast and come cruising up behind you. Make sure to get over and shout "wheelchair" to the people ahead of you as a heads-up.

☐ **Don't wear your race shirt.** New York City's longest streaker imparted this wisdom: "There's still a general rule among older runners that you don't wear the race shirt. If it's a marathon in 2020, you don't wear the 2020 shirt in the race. You have to finish the race to be entitled to wear the shirt." It's akin to not wearing a concert shirt to the concert. Feel free to wear old marathon shirts, however, for clout.

☐ **Step aside to walk.** Don't stop dead in your tracks in the middle of the road. It can cause accidents, and someone might run into you. If you have to stop or walk, head over to the side first.

☐ **Share the road.** This may be your first time running with strangers. Give everyone their space and don't clip a slower runner's heels. Look over your shoulder before moving, and if you're running alongside someone, feel free to strike up a conversation. For more information on sharing the course, see pages 110–111.

☐ **Use a port-o-john.** While a nice bush or fence might seem like an enticing place to take a leak (especially for guys, but I've seen women pop a squat too), wait for a port-o-john instead. Most races have plenty of them along the course, and marathons are family-friendly events full of individuals not looking to get flashed.

☐ **Take your time in the john.** While you're in the john, take your time. Some runners are in such a hurry that their aim is poor (from both ends). Take an extra few seconds to compose yourself before you go, so that the toilet is clean and usable for your fellow runners.

☐ **Keep your bib out.** Race officials need to be able to see your bib, so make sure it's visible. It's OK to have it covered for a mile or so while you warm up, but by Mile 3 it should be out. If you're wearing multiple layers, try pinning it to your shorts or rolling up your top layer so the bib is in plain sight. (Also, they identify you in pictures by your bib, so if they can't see it, you aren't getting those pics.)

☐ **Snot rocket to the side.** If you need to blow your nose, go to the side of the road and double check that no one is coming. No one wants your boogies on them. The same goes for hocking a loogie.

☐ **Thank the volunteers.** They're not getting paid and their hands are going to smell like Gatorade for weeks, so you might as well smile and say thanks!

Clockwise from top: Milano Marathon, Italy, 2016; Sydney Marathon, Australia, 2016; Rome Marathon, Italy, 2017 >>

MILE 10

Weather

Double digits baby! That's a milestone for you, and while the first few miles may have breezed by, you're going to start feeling things soon enough. One such thing: the weather.

Yes, I am aware that weather has been happening for you since before the race even started, but it takes the marathoning body some time to acclimate to whatever Zeus and his squad of mischievous cronies are throwing at you. For example, let's say it's raining. Waiting for the start, in the wee hours of the morning, you are *frigid*, but then the gun goes off and your body starts to heat up a bit. The sun peeks out. You're warming up a smidge. By Mile 10 in the rain, though, your body is probably not getting any warmer. This is the state that you'll be spending the next two-plus hours in. Plus, by Mile 10 your shoes are fully soaked and you can feel a chafe coming on. Now is the time to assess the situation. It's only going to get worse, so how are you going to get through? Conversely, if it's a scorcher, you might feel OK in the early going before the sun rears its scalding head. By Mile 10, though, you're for sure suffering.

Weather is a *big deal* in the marathon because you're going to be outside in the elements for, all things considered, three hours at the very least. You've got to have clothes ready for every weather scenario. If you don't bring a rain jacket or shorts because you "checked the forecast," you could be in for a world of hurt if the meteorologist messed up.

<< Boston Marathon, Massachusetts, USA, 2018

Famous Mile 10s

■ Of the hundreds of marathons hosted worldwide each year, six have been designated Abbott World Marathon Majors. The Tokyo Marathon, the first of the majors hosted each year, steers thousands of runners through the streets of Japan's capital. At the heart of the city is Skytree, the tallest tower in the world. At Mile 10 of the marathon, runners can spy the landmark rising above the city across the Sumida River.

■ Midwesterners looking for a marathon that is equal parts city and shoreline should sign up for the Milwaukee Marathon, run every April in Wisconsin. No sight in the city is more recognizable than the Milwaukee Art Museum, known to locals as the "Calatrava" in honor of the building's architect, Santiago Calatrava. Overlooking Lake Michigan, the museum's iconic white wings (which can open and close) oversee Mile 10 of the race.

■ Vermont may be one of the least-populated states in the Union, but that doesn't stop Vermonters from throwing one bumpin' marathon once a year in Burlington. The Vermont City Marathon leads runners not only along the coast of Lake Champlain and through the city's shady parks, but also up and down the city's historic Church Street. Wave to the drag queens cheering you on at Mile 10, and save room for Ben & Jerry's at the finish.

✓ BODY CHECK — Weather-Related Injuries

"The worst case is hot and humid," said Chicago Marathon Medical Director Dr. George Chiampas about race-day weather. While hot, sunny days bring the threat of dehydration, heat stroke, sunburn, and overheating, they are not the only dangerous running conditions. Purely cold days (below freezing but no snow) increase the risk of frostbite, hypothermia, and injuries inflicted by cold muscles. Hypothermia is even more ominous on cold, wet days when wet clothes and shoes cling to your body. Wet clothes also bring chafing, blisters, and bleeding. The best way to avoid weather-related injuries is to plan ahead. Look at the forecast and wear clothes that suit the occasion. If you're caught off-guard midrace, stop off at an aid tent, where they will have sunscreen and fluids for the heat, and they can help you dry off and warm up in the cold. If precipitation is on the docket, be careful to avoid slipping and wiping out, which can cause long-term injuries (looking at you, broken hip.) And while marathons are typically canceled in the event of lightning, hurricanes, or tornados, your training runs won't be, so don't be a hero. If there's a possibility of being electrocuted or blown across the state, postpone your run. It's better to skip a day than to end up in traction. ■

heat index: an index that combines temperature and humidity to determine how it *feels*

While your iPhone weather app may tell you it's 80 degrees out, the National Weather Service's heat index will let you know that the 90 percent humidity makes it feel like it's 102 degrees. However, it is often overlooked that the heat index gives you the perceived temperature *in the shade*. That means that out in direct sunlight, the perceived temperature is much higher. Whether you're on a long training run or in an actual marathon, the

heat index is something to be keenly aware of. While 68 degrees is a beautiful temperature for a lazy afternoon stroll, if it's humid and you're running down a stretch of highway (a marathon staple), it could feel like it's in the upper 80s.

"If I hadn't checked the heat index before my run, I would have ended up sucking water from a stranger's sprinkler."

"Weather is a big deal in the marathon because you're going to be outside in the elements for three hours at the very least."

▪ ▪ ▪ ▪

Running along with Boston Marathon Champion *Des Linden*

While we're in the bad weather chapter, let's call an expert in the field—professional marathoner Des Linden. Des has run in two Olympics and currently has a personal record of 2:22:38. She also won the Boston Marathon (the first American woman to do so in 33 years) during a horrific storm, noted as one of the worst in the race's history. Coming out of college, Des didn't even want to run marathons. She told her coach, "I'm going to do the 10K, that's it." But while volunteering at the finish line of the Chicago Marathon in 2006, she caught the bug. Today, she's one of the scrappiest runners in the United States. I sat down to pick her brain on running in the elements.

Your first marathon was Boston in 2007. Can you tell me a little about that experience?

[The Boston Marathon] was a US championship that year, and having elite marks in the half-marathon, 10K, etc., they let me into the field as part of the US championships. I loved it. It was a pretty nasty weather day.

There was a nor'easter, a big storm coming in, and the race organizers actually had threatened to cancel it a couple times. It was just going to be too bad for people to run in. Obviously, it went off without a hitch. Most people were miserable. I finished and was like, "That's the best thing I've ever done. I'm so hooked on this!" I was pretty oblivious to the conditions being bad because it was so fun.

When you won Boston in 2018, the weather was notoriously bad as well. How did that affect your race?

I think it levels the playing field a little bit. It rewards gritty runners and people who have a really good race plan, and the smartest runner can take advantage of those conditions because mistakes are magnified in bad conditions.

How does knowing a race is going to be in bad weather affect your mindset?

I think a lot of people let it get in their heads and they overthink it and worry too much. Yeah, it's going to be bad, but if you can reframe it and use it as a positive, it changes your entire day. I was really able to do that. It makes decisions on the course a lot more important, like moves or covering things or staying with the pack to avoid the wind. Those decisions all become a little more critical.

How do you train to run in races like that?

I really don't avoid [bad weather days in training]. Being in Michigan, we get pretty much all of it. [Boston 2018] was a bad day, but it's not the worst thing I've ever run in. Michigan has thrown a lot more at me.

What is the worst weather you've ever run in?

It was a "feels like" minus-30 degrees that came with a storm and some wind. I was out there running in that just to get in my regular training miles, but it's all better than the treadmill. It's all relative.

What is one tip or trick for running marathons that you'd give to a first-time marathoner?

I wish there was a secret, but the thing that people hate to hear about the marathon is that the advice is to be patient. It takes 10 years to become an overnight success, and you have to show up every day and put in the work and not expect to see a result tomorrow. Expect to see the result in three months when you get to the start line. Once you're racing, it's the same thing. It's 26.2 miles, and you have to be patient for 24 of them and then be tough for the rest. It's the worst piece of advice because it's hard to take.

Maintenance

As the miles continue to tick on, the topic of maintenance arises. The decisions you made at the start of the race regarding equipment, fueling, and clothes are starting to have consequences. Take, for example, your shoes. Did you tie them too tight? Did you single-knot them and notice they're beginning to loosen? Are your socks causing a weird rub? If the answer to any of those questions is yes, now is the time to pull over to the side quickly and straighten it out. You're at the point in the race where retying your shoes will only take a couple seconds. In another 10 miles, your feet could be in a world of hurt and handling the crisis will take triple the time due to fatigue.

Some other things to check on while you're still fresh: Any clothes rubbing in weird places? Do you need to use the restroom? Are you drinking enough water? Do you need a gel? Most problems are still fixable at this point. Aid stations often hand out Vaseline for chafing and water or gels if you need them. A med tent can tape those nipples or throw a Band-Aid on a hot spot. If you wear clothes (or a trash bag) that you're willing to discard along the course, you can take off layers as needed. You can also give a friend an extra hat or jacket to hand you if you're getting cold when you see them along the way.

Marathoners go into the marathon with a game plan, which is great—you need one—but you've also got to be flexible. This is a sporting event that throws a lot at its players. You've got to be in tune with your body and able to make adjustments on the fly. What worked in your last race might not work now, but know that there is still time, even two hours in, to fix problems.

<< London Marathon, England, 2009 **Pages 100–101:** London Marathon, England, 2010

✔ BODY CHECK — The Knees

When you talk to runners about injuries, the knees get a lot of attention. Marathon coach Greg McMillan explains why: "Most runners are taking 35,000 to 45,000 steps across the marathon. So, if you think of hopping on one leg 20,000 times in a row, that's what the marathon demands." By Mile 11, each knee has already sustained nearly 5,000 blows. The long-term wear and tear on knees depends on numerous factors, but here are some things to know.

1. Strengthening leg muscles decreases the strain on the knee and your chances of incurring the dreaded runner's knee, which is caused by inflammation of the cartilage under your kneecap. So work out those hamstrings, calves, quads, and glutes. While you can and should consult a trainer for more specific exercises, here are a few to start with:

■ **Lunges:** Lunges are a great place to begin. Use them in a variety of directions to strengthen your thigh muscles.

■ **One-legged squats:** One-legged squats not only work your quads and glutes, but also exercise the finer muscles in your feet and increase balance, all of which help in running.

■ **Calf raises:** As the connection between the knee and the ankle, the calf muscle is an important stabilizer, so strengthening it when not running is key.

■ **Crunches:** The core is the gateway to the entire body, so *work it out*!

2. Running on level ground decreases the risk of a knee (or ankle) injury caused by twisting or pulling, especially if you've got weak leg muscles.

3. The more weight you're carrying, the more strain on your knees (gravity is a cruel mistress), so lightening the load can lead to happier joints.

4. If you've already got knee injuries (thanks, high school football!), using a knee brace could be the way to go. It will limit knee movement, decreasing the risk of something popping out of place on your 20,000-hop journey. ■

Famous Mile 11s

■ Few races check off more historic landmarks than the Rome Marathon, which directs runners past the ruins of Ancient Rome's Forum and Circus Maximus as well as the city's Olympic Stadium from 1960. At Mile 11, the route bumps up against Vatican City so that runners can spot St. Peter's Basilica, the famed Catholic church within the papal state. Hopefully Pope Francis is praying for your knees.

■ The number one reason to run the New Orleans Marathon is to wolf down beignets before and after the race. The second is the course, which winds through many of the city's historic neighborhoods, including the French Quarter during Mile 11. Run through the city's oldest sector, listening to live jazz music as you cross Bourbon Street. If you're lucky, someone might throw you a set of Mardi Gras beads!

■ "If running up hills slows you down, then why not eliminate the uphill climb?" asked the creators of the World's Fastest Marathon. The race, located in the Sierra Nevada mountain range in Spain, is nearly 100 percent downhill, with an overall altitude drop of more than 6,000 feet. Looking for a PR (personal record) or BQ (Boston qualifier)? This race is for you. And Mile 11? All downhill.

MARATHON VOCAB WORD

foam roller:

a cylinder of compressed foam used by runners to loosen stiff muscles and aid in stretching

After long runs those leg muscles can get *stiff*. If you don't want to limp around the office (so embarrassing) or tear a muscle (less embarrassing?), you should be rolling. Pick which body part you'd like to focus on and then lay on top of the roller so it is between the sore body part and the ground. Then roll slowly until you find a tender, sore, or stiff muscle. Roll back and forth, massaging this spot with the foam until you feel the muscle loosen up. Calves, hamstrings, and hips are common areas of tightness for runners, but after long runs, the lower back, shoulders, and neck often need a roll too.

"I didn't have time to use my foam roller yesterday, and now I feel like the Tin Man."

▪ ▪ ▪ ▪
Racing along with Wheelchair Racing Extraordinaire *Amanda McGrory*

Before the elite runners even leave the starting corral at major marathons, a captivating high-stakes race is already underway. I'm talking, of course, about the wheelchair marathon, an event that Amanda McGrory knows quite well. Amanda—who was diagnosed with transverse myelitis, a spinal cord disorder, at the age of five—is a wheelchair athlete. After starting out as a wheelchair basketball player, Amanda transitioned to track and eventually the marathon, where she has been cleaning up since 2006. She has won seven Paralympic medals, including a gold in the 5,000M in Beijing and two marathon medals. She has also won the London, New York City, Los Angeles, and Tokyo Marathons in her long career of medal-podium finishes.

How did you decide to compete in your first marathon?

I was bribed. In 2006, my sophomore year of college, I was pretty frustrated with wheelchair racing. I wanted to be a middle-distance athlete. I was putting in the training and not getting any faster. In an attempt to keep me engaged, my coach told me he was hosting an elite track camp in Georgia. He told me the camp organizers wanted me to come, but they were being pretty picky with who they were inviting. They would make an

exception for me if I would agree to run a marathon in Colorado. His friend, who was in charge of the wheelchair division, was trying to build a field and had a hard time pulling people together. The deal was I was going to run the inaugural Colfax Marathon, and if I happened to win any prize money—most likely I wouldn't and I wouldn't do very well—then I would donate that money back to the camp.

So how did the marathon go?

I flew out to Denver, ran my first marathon, went 2:02, and finished third, but it was terrible. It was at altitude. The last nine miles of the course at the time were a climb, and there was a 400-meter stretch of grass in the middle. It was probably the worst first marathon I could have ever done. My second marathon was Grandma's in Duluth, Minnesota. It was about a month and a half later. I won the race, took 17 minutes off my time, and came within seconds of the course record. That is how my marathon career began!

You're covering the same distance as marathon runners, but obviously it's a very different sport. Can you tell me what the strategy is like?

I once heard wheelchair racing described as a hybrid of running, cycling, and speedskating. It's like running because it's the closest equivalent we have to running, and it's a direct power transfer. We don't have any gears like you have on a bike. It's like cycling because it's lower impact. We're not making direct contact with the ground. And it's like speedskating because you glide. One of the really cool things about wheelchair racing, particularly at the marathon distance, is that it's really dynamic because there are so many tactics that go into it. In running, for the most part athletes have a pace and try to stick to it and go a steady 26 miles. In wheelchair racing—because it's pack racing and there's a drafting effect— there are a lot more speed changes, lead changes, and attacks. And we're also more affected by outside factors. Wind plays a huge role, as well as road conditions, climbs, ascents, descents, and the strengths and weaknesses of the people around you. Throughout the race, every single person is trying to run the best race for them and the worst race for their competitors. Speeds drop down to 11 or 12 miles per hour for steep climbs. Downhill, the best coasters can get upward of 50 to 60 miles per hour. There are all these crazy speed changes and everybody is trying to set up their attacks, so you've got people sprinting up hills. You've got people taking supersharp fast corners. You never really know what's going to happen. Plus, there are crashes. Crashes are always exciting.

Mile 11

BQ's MARATHON HISTORY
A Marathoner on Wheels

Though Bob Hall lost the use of his legs after contracting polio before he was even a year old, he didn't see why needing a wheelchair should stop him from athletic competition. In 1974, Hall won the first wheelchair marathon in Toledo, Ohio. The following year, at age 23, he registered for the Boston Marathon, where Race Director Will Cloney told Hall he needed to complete the route in less than three hours for an official finish. Hall crossed the line in 2:58 to collect his Boston Athletic Association finisher's certificate and make Boston the first major marathon with a wheelchair division. By 1978, Hall had designed his first racing wheelchair and founded a company, Hall's Wheels, which outfits many racers today with sleek, aerodynamic, and ergonomically advanced designs that weigh half that of his original chair. Hall's 1986 racing chair design is part of the permanent collection of New York's Museum of Modern Art.

"One of the really cool things about wheelchair racing . . . is that it's really dynamic because there are so many tactics that go into it."

What's the training like?

That's another area where we differ from runners. Back in the late 1980s and early 1990s, someone figured out that if you train long, steady runs like runners do, you can go 26 miles at 15 miles per hour, but if you don't train starts and sprints and excels, you might run into a situation where, in a pack race, somebody will take off and attack and because you've been training steady, you've got nothing to give there. We do eight to 10 sessions a week, and we're usually in our racing chairs six days a week. We tend to be a little heavier on the mileage than a lot of runners. We do 100-plus miles during our heavy training. As far as physical recovery, like stress on your joints, it's a lot less because it's lower impact, so it's really just managing fatigue. That's why we do Boston and London back to back every year. We'll fly to Boston, race Boston on Monday, and then on Tuesday morning, we'll fly to London and race that one six days later.

Can you tell me a little bit about equipment you use and how that factors into the race?

There are certainly opportunities for things to go wrong, and getting a new racing chair is kind of like getting a new pair of shoes. Even if they are the exact same brand, size, and style, they're not going to feel the same as the pair you've been running in for the past six months, so getting a new racing chair is always a bit nerve-racking. I'd say the biggest risks during the race are always punctures and flat tires. If you're diligent and take care of your equipment, there is little risk for anything to go wrong, but we really have no control of what's on the road. When you're moving fast and hitting debris, potholes, or broken pavement, it can bust your tires and damage your chair.

How often do you switch out chairs?

I am sponsored by Honda, and I get a new chair every year from the company. As far as costs go, racing chairs can be $20,000 to $30,000. Even a base-model chair, with an aluminum frame and standard carbon-fiber wheels, is probably going to cost close to $5,000, so if you're paying out of pocket, it can be a very expensive sport.

What is one misconception people have about wheelchair marathoners?

I think this is for Paralympic sports as a whole. It has really come a long way as far as public recognition and understanding that we are in fact elite athletes, putting in hundreds of miles a week, training 10 sessions a week, building careers, and living off the prize money and sponsorships and endorsements we have as athletes. We're professional athletes just like anyone else.

Sharing the Course

While marathon runners may think the marathon is all about them, there are often multiple other types of people competing out on the racecourse in various events. Here's a quick primer on the other types of competitors you may see on race day.

☐ **Half-Marathoners:** Most marathons also host half-marathons. Some, like Detroit, have two separate half-marathons within the same marathon course! While the half-marathon course may be the same as the marathon, or may branch off, you have a high likelihood of seeing some halfers.

☐ **Relay Runners:** Many marathons also host relays, where teams of anywhere from two to more than 10 people run different legs of the race. You see someone cruising by you in the last few miles of the marathon? Most likely they've just jumped in for that final 5K on fresh legs. Some races distinguish those runners in the half-marathon or relay with a different colored bib, but it can be hard to tell when you're running.

☐ **Wheelchair Racers:** These athletes, whether in their normal wheelchairs or racing chairs, typically start first. Instead of using their legs, they use their arms to power them through 26.2. While they can coast on downhills, they've got to lug their chair uphill while trying not to roll backward.

☐ **Running Guides:** Since running a marathon often involves weaving around competitors and twisting through the city's streets, the visually impaired often run with guides. The individuals are typically tethered to their differently abled compatriots to steer them safely to the finish line.

☐ **Dogs:** What would man be without his best friend? While pets are prohibited in many races, some smaller marathons and trail runs are open to canine competitors.

☐ **Handcyclists:** Handcycles are different from wheelchairs in that they use pedals and gears much like a regular bicycle, but instead of using your legs, you use your arms for power. There has been some controversy as to whether handcyclists should be allowed to compete in marathons, or whether they should compete in cycling races. Handcycles are significantly faster than wheelchairs. Amanda McGrory, who wrote an op-ed on the topic for the *Boston Globe*, said, "They're two totally different sports. It would be like you running the Tour de France. That's insane. It's really confusing, especially for spectators, when they see somebody flying through on a handcycle covering 26 miles in under an hour, and then wheelchair athletes are still out there for an hour and 45 minutes."

☐ **Strollers:** While not technically a separate event, you will see strollers out on the course from time to time. Some marathons allow actual baby strollers on the course, while others do not. Most, however, allow one runner to push a person in a wheelchair or stroller. Team Hoyt is a well-known father-son pairing in which Dick Hoyt pushes his son Rick in a special wheelchair because he has cerebral palsy and can't run himself.

☐ **Rollerbladers:** The Berlin Marathon includes a whole section for inline skaters, making it a bucket-list event for blading aficionados. With the ability to coast, they can finish much faster than runners, although their likelihood of crashing is also much higher. So, if you worked at Sonic in high school and need a new place to use your skills, head to Germany.

MILE 12

Course Shapes

You're getting close to the halfway point, which means, in many marathons (such as Chicago, Baltimore, or Detroit), you're headed back downtown. The half-marathoners are about to finish, the crowds are ramping back up, and the skyscrapers are hovering overhead.

But not all marathons double back in that way. Some marathons are big loops or point to point, which basically means a meandering line. While 26.2 is always 26.2, the shape of the marathon course can affect your race in a big way, so let's look at some of the pros and cons.

One of the most common forms is the clover-shaped course, which doubles back near the starting line multiple times. These courses accommodate the half-marathoners (who make up a large chunk of most marathons), but also are great for spectators. Usually they can see their runner four or five times without moving around too much. Clover-shaped courses also allow the city to showcase its downtown multiple times, so all in all this is a pretty runner-friendly type of course.

Another popular option is the loop-shaped course, which allows runners to start and finish in the same place (easy parking), but allows runners to go a little farther afoot. The Walt Disney World Marathon, which aims to hit all four parks, and the Houston Marathon, which winds through lots of cool neighborhoods, both employ this shape. There's more visual interest, but it's harder for spectators without a car and wonky for half-marathoners.

And then there's the classic point-to-point course, invented in Ancient Greece and today used mostly in major races that don't accommodate halves—such as New York, Los Angeles, Boston, and London. Parking is annoying if you don't have a friend for drop-off and pickup, but you can *go places*. Psychologically, the journey is also very satisfying.

All marathon shapes (and marathoners!) are beautiful, but you should definitely plan accordingly.

<< Stramilano Marathon, Italy, 2012

Marathon Course Shapes

Marathons come in all shapes and sizes. Here are some examples of the many forms the 26.2 miles can take.

- **Vienna City Marathon (Spiral Course):** Run two circles of the downtown, moving closer and closer to the center.

- **Bayshore Marathon (Out and Back):** Run out 13.1 miles and back the way you came. This is the only style of course that lets you see every single one of your competitors.

- **Fenway Park Marathon (Multiple Loop):** Run the same small course 116.5 times in a row. While some find it monotonous, others love the repetition, and you'll know Boston's famed baseball stadium extremely well.

- **Boston Marathon (Point to Point):** Start 26.2 miles away from the finish in this straight shot of a marathon. It offers great visual interest for runners, but it's difficult for spectators and parking.

- **Berlin Marathon (Loop):** Start and end in the same park, running a huge circuit of the city in between.

- **San Francisco Marathon (Loop with Bridge):** Run a wide loop of the city with a there-and-back across the Golden Gate Bridge at Mile 7.

- **Chicago Marathon (Clover-Shaped Loop):** This course is great for spectators, who can catch runners at multiple points as they run in and out of downtown four times.

- **Vermont City Marathon (Clover-Shaped Loop):** Return within a half mile of the start five times in this true clover that has you retracing your steps several times.

- **Dubai Marathon (Multiple-Loop There and Back):** Run two miniature there-and-back courses (the second loop twice!) in a course that maximizes the distance without shutting down loads of roads.

- **New York City Marathon (Five-Borough Point to Point):** To hit all five boroughs, you'll run in a straight line for most of the course before doubling back to Central Park from the Bronx.

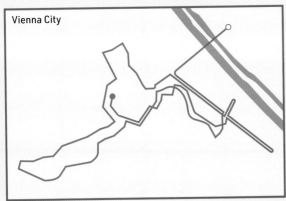

Vienna City

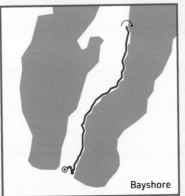

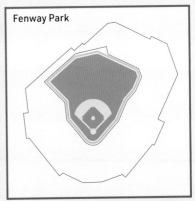

Bayshore

Fenway Park

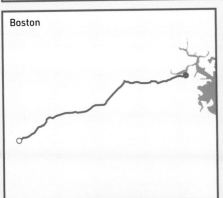

Boston

Berlin

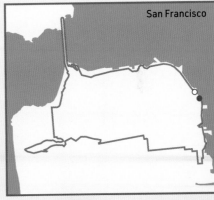

San Francisco

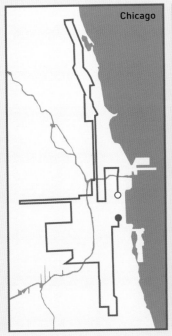

Chicago

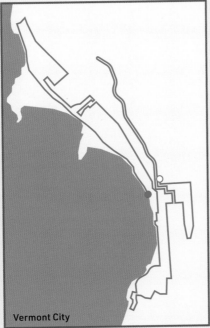

Vermont City

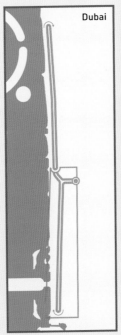

Dubai

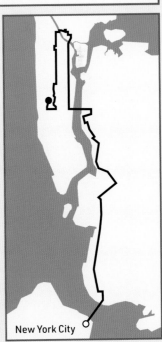

New York City

✔️ BODY CHECK — Ideal Running Form

We've been at this for 12 miles, which means the temptation to jettison good habits is increasing. One habit often left by the wayside is good running form. Dr. Mark Cucuzzella has just the trick to keep you focused. "Sometimes I'll write these initials on my fingers," he says, "for whenever I get into a bad space." The initials are:

- ◼ **P for Posture:** Stand tall.
- ◼ **B for Breath:** Abdominal breathing will help reset your posture.
- ◼ **R for Relax:** It's easy to relax when your breathing is under control.
- ◼ **S for Spring:** Those feet shouldn't be thudding along.

Curt Munson, who helmed the running store Playmakers for 30-plus years and taught Good Form Running classes, adds two more keys to ideal running form:

- ◼ **M for Midfoot:** Try to take small steps and land on the middle of your foot rather than the heel.
- ◼ **L for Lean:** Run with a slight forward lean to your body.

If you rearrange the letters, you'll get the easy acronym PRBLMS (posture, relax, breath, lean, midfoot, and spring). If you've got problems, think of PRBLMS. (Yes, I'm rather proud of coining this phrase!) ◼

Famous Mile 12s

■ It's just like being a movie star! You, running down Hollywood Boulevard while thousands of onlookers cheer and take pictures. Except that you're sweaty, and they have no idea who you are. But Mile 12 of the Los Angeles Marathon is still magical. You're running past the Hollywood Walk of Fame and Grauman's Chinese Theatre, you're on your way to the Santa Monica Pier, and, most years, there is at least one B-list celebrity running somewhere in the pack with you.

■ Most people head to South Carolina's Myrtle Beach for a relaxing vacation, but there's no better time to relax than after pounding out 26.2 miles, right? The Myrtle Beach Marathon, run each March, consists of one giant loop of the city that allows runners miles worth of ocean views. At Mile 12, you'll run past the beach's massive Ferris wheel, SkyWheel, towering over the tourist town. Maybe catch a ride after the run?

■ We've all heard of cities so far north that during summer it never gets dark. Such is the case in Tromsø, Norway, home of the Midnight Sun Marathon and third-largest city north of the Arctic Circle. The race, which begins at 8:30 p.m., is run completely in daylight despite finishers coming in after midnight. At Mile 12, as you cross the Tromsø Bridge over the Tromsøysundet Strait, you'll still be able to work on your tan.

MARATHON VOCAB WORD

Strava: a social media app for runners that is used to track runs and share progress with friends

It's like Instagram, except instead of sharing pictures, you're sharing your runs (or bike rides and swims, but we're not focused on those). Using the GPS in your phone or smartwatch, Strava tracks your runs, keeping a record of your mileage and splits. The app serves as both a runner's journal and a way to connect with fellow running enthusiasts. For the vain, the app is a great form of peer pressure. Increase your mileage or lower your splits to impress all your runner friends. Periodic challenges on the app provide added incentives to pound the pavement on days you feel like staying in.

"I felt lazy on Tuesday, but then my crush added me on Strava so I ran 10 miles to impress her."

Running along with New York City Marathon Founder *George Hirsch*

In the world of New York running, it's hard to find someone who's more integral than George Hirsch. George describes himself as a "magazine man first and foremost," which is certainly true. He founded *New York* magazine and *The Runner*, a competitor of the now-prominent *Runner's World*, before the two merged in 1987. When the two publications joined, George became the publisher. To describe him only as a "magazine man," though, would be a great disservice. George also helped found the New York City Marathon, now the largest marathon in the world. He's also a television marathon commentator who has covered three Olympics in addition to races like Boston and New York. He has run 40 marathons himself and even met his wife at a marathon. Now 85, George serves as the chairman of the board of the New York Road Runners, the organization that hosts the marathon each year. He is also an excellent storyteller. Here are a few of George's memories from over the years.

You helped found the New York City Marathon back in 1970. Can you paint a picture of how all that happened?

I was already a marathon runner by the time the first New York City Marathon came in 1970 in Central Park. Fred Lebow [cofounder and longtime organizer of the marathon] and I were very close friends. When he started it, I have to confess the idea of running those loops in the park did not appeal to me. Boston was the only game in town, and for that first marathon in New York, there were pedestrians, bikes, and people weaving in and out. There was no way to organize anything or any logistical support. It was enough to get some numbers and safety pins. I didn't want to spend my time training for those races in the park.

But everything changed in 1976. Back then, there wasn't such a thing as a big-city marathon. The Boston Marathon started 20 miles outside the city. There was a New York runner named George Spitz, who was this wonderfully offbeat character. He'd say, "We've got to do a marathon through the five boroughs." I would humor him and say, "Sure, George, sounds interesting." Fred would say, "Forget it, George. What you're talking about could cost $15,000, and where are we going to get that kind of money?"

George had a great Rolodex, and he got a local politician named Percy Sutton on board with the idea. Percy convinced some very influential real estate guys to put up some money, and then Percy, Fred, and I went down to see Mayor Abe Beame. The city was on the verge of bankruptcy and crime was sky-high. We came in and said we should do a five-borough marathon to celebrate the bicentennial of the United States and help lift the spirits of the city. At the end, the mayor agreed.

From then on, Fred found his calling in life. He began to put it together. He was a promoter at heart, and he knew he needed one person—Frank Shorter, who had won the Olympic championship in the marathon. Frank

agreed to run, and we got Bill Rodgers to agree as well. We did one press conference outside the Tavern on the Green because we didn't have the money for coffee and bagels for the press. The mayor and Frank came, and we got the story we wanted.

I ran the first citywide marathon, and I remember crossing over into Brooklyn and seeing crowds on either side of the street and thinking, "Oh my gosh." We never looked back. We never talked to the mayor about year two. We never asked about a permanent New York City Marathon. The first one was such a hit! There were 2,000 runners—100 of them were women—and it was *already bigger than Boston. It was the biggest marathon in the world, and after that any self-respecting city had to have a marathon. Everything in the world of marathoning changed.*

How has marathon journalism changed over the years?

Before The Runner, *people mostly wrote about race results. When we started the magazine, we started bringing in more professional journalists and hiring really good photographers. We were changing the whole game, writing long-form journalism that had a narrative, scene setting, and dialogue, yet was nonfiction. It was a different way of looking at it. It caught on, and stories were no longer just about who won the Cherry Blossom 10-Miler and what their time was. People really liked it. Now the question is where we are heading, as print is in major decline. Long-form journalism isn't what people are looking for now. People don't go on their phones to read a couple thousand words.*

What is your most memorable marathon?

My best marathon was easily the New Jersey Waterfront Marathon in 1988. At that point, I was publisher of Runner's World, *and I'd agreed to do commentary for the Olympic Games, which were in Seoul that year.*

The day before the race there was an expo. I was at the Runner's World *booth, and this very beautiful woman walked by. We looked at each other for a second, and then she just kept on walking. I said, "Hello," and she said, "Are you George Hirsch?" I would have said yes no matter who she asked for. A mutual friend had asked me six months before if I would send a training plan to a friend, which wasn't that unusual, and it turned out to be her. She said, "You sent me the training plan, and I followed it, and tomorrow is my first marathon." We talked and I said, "How would you like to have dinner with me tonight?" She said, "Well, no, I can't," but to keep the conversation prolonged, I walked her out to her car.*

The next morning, I had a big breakfast and then went to the race. By now, my mind was only focused on one thing. My reason for being there became somewhat secondary. So I walked into this sea of people, where looking for someone is impossible. The gun went off, and I couldn't find her. I waited for everyone to cross the starting line, and I started to jog and pass people on the right and left. I kept looking and looking and, sure enough, five miles into the marathon, I saw Shay up ahead of me. I came up alongside her, trying to be ever so cool. I said, "Hi," and she was like, "What are you doing here?" I said, "Actually, I was looking for you." We started to talk and share life stories. Three hours, 37 minutes, and one second later, she crossed the finish line. The next year, I married her.

"It was the biggest marathon in the world, and after that any self-respecting city had to have a marathon."

MILE 13 People Who Run

So far, we've spent a lot of time focusing on you, the runner, and the race, but if you'll look around quickly, there are thousands of other people out on the course. Marathons are unique in their massive size (what other sport allows 50,000 people to compete at once?), their diversity (all ages, genders, and abilities are welcome), and being one of the only sports where you can go out and compete with the best (you'd need an obscene amount of money to play basketball with LeBron James).

I ran a half-marathon in college and thought, "Well, that's it for me. I could never do a full marathon. Those are for young athletes, not normal people." When I moved to New York City a few years later, I watched the marathon live because it was an excuse to eat bagels and hang out with friends. I was *shocked* by how normal the runners were. Sure, the elites were effervescent gazelles with prominent abs, but otherwise the runners just looked like everyone from the mall dressed in athleisure. There were people of all shapes and sizes and ages, people pushing strollers, people with artificial limbs, people in costumes, people in wheelchairs, and even people who were pregnant! I thought, "Everyone can run a marathon, and I want to be a part of everyone."

Meb Keflezighi told me people stop him on the street and say, "I am also an immigrant. Thank you for all you have done for the community of immigrants to uplift us." The marathon is a sport for everyone to enjoy both as a runner and a fan. In life, we may all be different, but on race day, we've all got the same goal and we're all in it together.

split: the time it takes to run a specific distance, usually a smaller part of a longer race

Especially when running longer distances (like, say, a marathon), it is important to keep track of your split times. You may track mile-by-mile splits, or larger chunks of time, like 5K splits or half-marathon splits. Ideally, runners should keep a consistent pace for the entire race (or perhaps speed up in the last few miles if they've got energy left in the tank). Tracking splits allows you to see where you're lagging and where you're exerting too much energy. If your splits get increasingly slow, you're pushing too hard at the beginning of a run. If your splits vary wildly, then you might want to focus on pacing. George W. Bush said about his marathon, "I ran the first mile in 8:30 and the last mile in 8:30." Those are some mighty fine splits.

"I was sucking air for those last few miles, and my splits were a hot mess. I need to start slower next time."

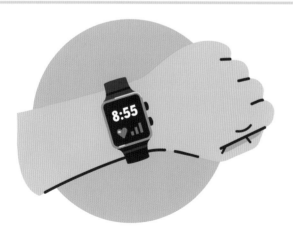

Famous Mile 13s

■ I don't remember much from my running of the Baltimore Marathon because I had received a concussion that I was unaware of the night before. What I do remember is running through the city's famed Inner Harbor at Mile 13 of the course. Runners pass huge crowds of fans in the city's beautiful downtown before heading back out on the course's second loop.

■ Few American landmarks are more recognizable than St. Louis's Gateway Arch, perched on the banks of the Mississippi River and beckoning travelers westward. The city's marathon smartly crosses in front of the national park (established in 2018) at Mile 13 before eventually finishing in the arch's shadow.

■ Another of the Abbott World Marathon Majors, the London Marathon is not short on impressive landmarks. Runners pass by Big Ben, the London Eye, and St. Paul's Cathedral, but perhaps the most impressive feature of the course is running across the city's iconic Tower Bridge (not to be confused with the much less exciting London Bridge) at Mile 13.

■ It's hard to find a marathon experience more moving than the 13th mile of the Marine Corps Marathon in Washington, DC. As runners pass through the "Wear Blue Mile," they'll first encounter the photos of fallen servicemen and women. Then, as they approach Hains Point, the posters give way to cheering volunteers, each bearing an American flag representing one of the fallen heroes. It's poignant and powerful!

✔ BODY CHECK—Sunburn

Back at 4:00 a.m., when you were getting ready for your marathon, sunburn was not top of mind (it was freezing!). Now that you're at Mile 13, however, and have been running in the sun for two hours, you're going to wish you'd lathered on the SPF. Marathoning is an outdoor sport, and four-plus hours in the sun (even on a cloudy day) can be dangerous for your skin. In addition to being painful, sunburns also lead to increased body temperature, which can cause dehydration and other horrors. Some solutions: Wear sunscreen, but put it on at least 20 minutes before you run so it can absorb into your skin. Try running with a hat or T-shirt to block some of those nasty UV rays. Although you don't have much say in the race itself, for training runs, pick shady paths and run early or late to avoid the worst from the sun. A nice tan is fine, but skin cancer is a no-go. ■

BQ's MARATHON HISTORY
An Ethiopian Marathoner? That's New!

Born in the mountains of Ethiopia on the same day as the 1932 Olympic Marathon, Abebe Bikila may have been destined for marathon greatness. Ethiopia was occupied by Italy for much of Bikila's childhood, but by age 20 he'd joined the Imperial Bodyguard of the returned Ethiopian emperor. And 25 years after the invasion of his country, Bikila ran a marathon—barefoot—through the cobblestone streets of Rome at the 1960 Olympics. His run included crossing the Piazza Venezia, where Benito Mussolini had declared the Italian campaign against Ethiopia, and kicking into a final sprint at a fourth-century Ethiopian obelisk that had been looted 25 years earlier by Italian soldiers. When Bikila crossed the line in 2:15:16.2, he set a new marathon world record and became the first black African to win an Olympic gold medal. Four years later, in Tokyo, he would win again, the first back-to-back winner of the Olympic Marathon, this time in Pumas.

■ ■ ■ ■
Running along with Writer *Lindsay Crouse*

There's your typical marathon reporting (who won, their time, etc.), and then there's what Lindsay Crouse does. The journalist—who works in the *New York Times* op-doc department (that's short for opinion-documentaries, basically short nonfiction films)—has also made a niche for herself writing thoughtful long-form pieces on marathon and running culture. She broke the story of Nike's lack of maternity support for the athletes it sponsors. She detailed how Shalane Flanagan's rise brought a new wave of American female marathoners with her. A marathoner herself, she also documented her attempt to qualify for the 2020 Olympic Trials and the community of women she built along that journey. Here are some of her latest musings on the sport.

You work at the *New York Times*, but you weren't hired to cover running. How did you carve out this niche for yourself?

Positions have never really opened up for me. I've forged them myself, for lack of a better term, and I think that's exactly how distance running works too. You don't join a team and have a coach lay out your meets or races for you. You decide, and you go do it. You show up, and you're in charge of how well you do. Instead of looking at what jobs existed, I looked at where we didn't have jobs and where we weren't really reporting on things. After working here awhile, I realized I never read the sports pages because the articles weren't the way I looked at sports. Then I thought that was crazy because I'm an athlete! So I just started pitching stories. I wasn't piggybacking off a story that someone else had written; I was seeing something new and different. Women's sports are woefully undercovered, and they're woefully underreported by women. No one is asking me to do these stories, but I realized I needed to write about the sport through my own lens.

What trends are you seeing in marathon running now?

The sub-elite story of American women absolutely killing it right now, as opposed to ever before. Running together, connecting—it's all fascinating to me. I think it's the most important American athletic story that is going on right now. It is so exciting to see all these women, particularly at older ages, having these absolute breakthroughs when even four to eight years ago we would have turned 30 and said, "I peaked." Right now is a new heyday of American distance running, and it's led by females. I get a lot of personal and professional satisfaction from helping to drive that. Let's create these female athletic icons because they don't just happen on their own!

What is the weirdest marathon story you've ever encountered?

I'm very into jogglers [juggling joggers]. Joggling got banned at the New York City Marathon. I realized this the day before, pitched the story to my boss, and then from 8:00 p.m. to 5:00 a.m., I was on the phone with jogglers around the world. They all united to protest this ban. It was like writing candy.

What is one thing you've learned about running marathons from your experience writing about them?

There can be a certain amount of dogma when it comes to running, but people should be open to playing with those rules. The rules that other people make may not be best for me, and they may in some ways be holding me back if I'm trying to rigidly adhere to a standard that someone made for themselves and not for me.

What do you think about when you're running?

Running has made me think a lot about how you improve, what your limits are, and how you can change those limits. I think that's really the core of what a lot of people enjoy about running. It's not about the running itself. It's about what it represents. I feel bad for people who consider running to be solely a health and fitness initiative. There's so much more texture to it.

MILE 14

The Half-Marathon

13.1! For marathon runners, this marks the halfway point, but let's take a minute to celebrate the half-marathon. Jim Heim, the race director for the New York City Marathon, once said, "I wish we had come up with a better name for the half-marathon when it first launched. The word *half* makes it sound like half of something else, but it is quite an accomplishment in and of itself." I couldn't have said it better myself.

Just like a marathon is half of a 50-mile race, but still a tremendous achievement, so is the half-marathon. Thirteen miles, or more than two hours of straight running for many, is a massive undertaking. For nonrunners, even a mile can be grueling, so working up to 13 of them is mind-blowingly hard. It takes months of sweat, early morning and late-night runs, and foot blisters to get to this finish line.

So, if 13.1 is the end of your incredible running journey, *congratulations*! You're a boss! But, if you want to get crazy and push yourself even further, we've got nine-tenths more of this mile to finish off. And if you're thinking, "I barely finished the half; there is no way I could do two of those," you sure aren't alone. I think most marathoners have said that, but believe me: you can and you will.

<< Chicago Rock 'n' Roll Half-Marathon, Illinois, USA, 2017

✔ BODY CHECK — Cramping

Late in the race, your muscles are tired, torn, and easily susceptible to cramping. Cramps can strike at any time, but how and why? Marathon coach and exercise scientist Greg McMillan doesn't have the perfect answer. "Nobody has really figured out the cramp exactly," he says, "because it doesn't seem to always be related to the same thing." But he has nailed down some of the culprits:

■ **Dehydration:** If you don't hydrate properly before or during the race, your dehydrated muscles can start to seize up.

■ **No Fuel in the Tank:** Not intaking enough carbs before the race or calories (like gels) during the race can lead to low fuel stores, which lead to cramping.

■ **Low Salt:** If you're a salty sweater, you can lose sodium, an essential electrolyte, over a marathon and send your muscles into cramps.

■ **Anxiety:** Especially early in the race, cramps can be the result of anxiety. Getting into a relaxed headspace during the beginning of the race can relieve tension in your clenched muscles.

Marathon cramps can come from any combination of these factors, but Greg gives a lot of credit to the brain. If your brain senses a threat to your body (i.e., running 26.2 grueling miles), it will start sending distress signals to protect you. A cramp is an easy way to slow you down. So, while there is no surefire way to prevent muscle cramps, good mental and physical preparation can keep you from lying on the curb, pounding on your quads. ■

Famous Mile 14s

■ If you want to ascend the famed Pikes Peak in the Rockies and also run a marathon, you can now kill two birds with one stone. The Pikes Peak Marathon, run every year outside Colorado Springs, allows participants to race to the top of the 14er (coincidentally, Mile 14 includes the summit) along trails before running back down the mountain to the finish. It is one of the few races where the second half may be easier than the first.

■ Cue the *Big Little Lies* theme song because the halfway point of California's Big Sur Marathon is *the* bridge. Technically, it's called the Bixby Creek or Bixby Canyon Bridge, and technically it's a reinforced-concrete open-spandrel arch bridge. For our purposes, though, it's the bridge along the Pacific Ocean that Meryl Streep drove across in the opening credits of the HBO show while she wore false teeth.

■ The fourth of the Abbott World Marathon Majors, the Chicago Marathon is run every fall in the Windy City. Known for its flat course and exuberant midwestern fans, the Chicago Marathon repeatedly returns runners to the city's downtown. During Mile 14, marathoners run underneath Chicago's elevated trains network (or "the L" to locals) before crossing one of the city's recognizable drawbridges over the Chicago River.

MARATHON VOCAB WORD

elite: extremely fast, usually professional distance runner in competition to win high-profile marathons

Unlike most sports, where professional athletes are sectioned off in their own leagues far from amateur riffraff, the marathon has Olympians racing against Janet from accounting. The vast majority of marathoners have no shot at winning, however, so race organizers separate the actual contenders into their own tier labeled "elites." These runners, selected based on their previous times and accomplishments, start the race before the masses. While many elites are professional runners without a day job, fast amateurs can qualify for elite status in some marathons with fast PRs. In many races (such as New York and Chicago), elites wear bibs bearing their first or last names instead of numbers. It is also a tradition at many races for the year's previous male winner to wear the #1 bib while the previous female winner dons #101.

"I just want to be an elite so my bib says Huff instead of 25601."

■ ■ ■ ■

Running along with Half-Marathon King *Ryan Hall*

The aim for many first-time half-marathoners is just to crack two hours. Ryan Hall finished the 13.1 in half that, clocking in at 59:43 at the 2007 Houston Half-Marathon. He currently holds the record for the fastest American half-marathoner ever. He is also the only US runner with a sub-2:05 marathon, which he ran at the 2011 Boston Marathon. He has run two Olympic Marathons; is married to another professional marathoner, Sara Hall; and in 2017 completed the World Marathon Challenge, which has entrants running seven marathons on seven continents in seven days.

Can you tell me how you decided to run your first marathon in London in 2007, and a little about the experience?

It was actually in 2006, at the end of my first year as a pro runner in the 5K. I was on the track racing Kenenisa Bekele and Craig Mottram in London, and just getting tanked by those guys. I remember coming down the backstretch of that race and watching them finish on the jumbotron. I was thinking to myself, "Man, this is not how I pictured this going down. I pictured myself running with the best guys in the world, and I'm not even in the race." I'd won the US 12K title unexpectedly, and thought, "Hey, if I'm going to try out longer distances [marathons], and it seems like I'm better the longer I go, I should get going on it now with Beijing [the host of the 2008 Olympics] coming up." Things were just clicking for me in the longer distances, so I decided I'd debut at the Los Angeles Marathon in March 2007. I decided to run the Houston Half-Marathon as a check-in because my training had been going very well. I set the American record in the half-marathon, ran 59:43, and then the door just kind of opened to run with the best guys in the world at the London Marathon. I knew from the moment that I ran the first one, or maybe even before, during training, that this was going to be my event.

Tell me about breaking that one-hour mark in Houston?

I'd set the goal that one day I wanted to break an hour, but I'd still never run a half-marathon, so obviously I wasn't expecting it to happen during my first one. But there was something that really clicked for me as I transitioned over. Having focused on speed for so long, when I transitioned to longer stuff I was at my best because I had that 5K fitness in my back pocket. That day, I ran, got going, and the first mile was like 4:35, slightly slower than what I averaged but faster than I should have been going. I looked at my watch, and thought, "That felt really easy." I was surprised, excited, and shocked because I didn't think I'd finish in under an hour. I don't know if I was ever that fit again.

132   MARATHONER

Aside from the distance, what are the differences between running a marathon and a half-marathon?

The speed of the half-marathon is obviously a lot faster. What you're working on with distance running is your threshold, which just means a line you have where if you go any faster you're going to blow up and start going backward. I'd argue that if you're in your best half-marathon shape, it's impossible to also be in your best marathon shape because the thresholds are different.

What about nutrition for the two races?

There's a big difference. For half-marathons, you don't need to take in any calories. [Depending on your own speed and experience level, you may need to take in calories during the half-marathon.] You're not limited by nutrition in the half-marathon, whereas you are in the marathon because you're running up against that glycogen depletion. Hitting the wall doesn't happen in the half.

While significantly more people run halves, professionals often seem to skip over this distance for the marathon. Why is that?

The half-marathon is not in the Olympics, so if you want to go to the Olympics, you've got to do it in the marathon. The marathon definitely has more prestige, and there's also a financial factor for sure. [Marathon winners can earn up to six figures, while half-marathon winners often receive less than $1,000.]

Since retiring from running, you've started weight lifting. How has that change in your body type affected your running?

When I was running professionally, I was 5 feet, 10 inches, and 137 pounds. Now I'm 182 pounds. It feels 100 percent different. My movement does not feel as fluid. My stride feels small. You go from feeling like a gazelle to feeling like a rhino. I'm way more powerful, though, and I'm way faster sprinting!

"For nonrunners, even a mile can be grueling, so working up to 13 of them is mind-blowingly hard."

Wild and Wacky Halves

Because the marathon is such a long, arduous distance, races tend to be either standard road races or trail runs. With the half, though, race organizers sometimes get *very* inventive. Here are some of the craziest half-marathons you can participate in around the world.

The Santa Hustle (Sandusky, Ohio): Every December, thousands of people dress up as Santa Claus and run through the abandoned Cedar Point theme park that closes in October.

Wine Country Runs (Paso Robles, California): Run through California's vineyards in this booze-themed half. The winners win their weight in wine. Everyone else gets a free glass when they finish.

Havana Half-Marathon (Havana, Cuba): Run along the Caribbean waterfront and through the beautiful historic downtown in this tropical half.

500 Festival Mini-Marathon (Indianapolis, Indiana): Fans of the Indy 500 will love this race that features a lap through the Indianapolis Motor Speedway. Also, the aid stations are called "pits" for this race.

The Spartan Beast (Various Locations): Spartan's obstacle course races are tough. For the half, you must endure 30 obstacles, including jumping over fire, climbing walls, flipping tires, and crawling through mud.

Hershey Half-Marathon (Hershey, Pennsylvania): Run through America's chocolate capital (including the famed Hersheypark) to earn a candy-shaped medal and, of course, some chocolate.

Capital City River Run (Lansing, Michigan): Like I wasn't going to shout-out my hometown! Run through the Potter Park Zoo and the Michigan State University campus before ending at the state capitol building.

Mount Rushmore Half-Marathon (Keystone, South Dakota): The National Park Service hosts a number of scenic halves (Yellowstone, Grand Canyon, etc.), but this one has four ex-presidents cheering you on.

Star Wars Rival Run (Orlando, Florida): Disney offers a slew of themed halves. Star Wars characters line the course for this one, and you're welcome to rock Princess Leia buns as you weave through the parks.

Beer Half-Marathon (Various Locations): This is not technically a race, but brave alcohol lovers attempt this "beer a mile" race strategy. Just finishing is an accomplishment!

MILE 15

The Barren Second Half

As we enter the back half of the marathon, I'd like to touch down for a bit to discuss a phenomenon I like to call "the draining." While major marathons like New York, Boston, and London don't feature a half-marathon, most road races in the United States feature a massive pool of runners looking for that 13.1 bumper sticker. During Mile 14, those runners are siphoned off from the marathon, so by Mile 15, it's just the few, the proud, the marathoners.

And while all those cheery halfers are off to the bar, guess who is headed out with them? That's right, their friends and families, who were screaming so loudly 15 minutes ago. So now you're headed into the harder half of the race without the majority of the field and the fans, not to mention the fact that the marathoners are *very* spread out by now.

Thus, "the draining." The sheer population of the race has been drained and with it goes much of your adrenaline. During the first half you can coast along on the exuberance of the live event, but the second half becomes much more like a training run—just you grinding alone on the road. When it hit in my first marathon, I felt a massive deflation, so it's good to mentally prepare for the draining.

<< Jungfrau Marathon, Switzerland, 2011

Famous Mile 15s

■ Dun da da, dun da da, dun da da, dun da da. That's the score from *Rocky* if you couldn't figure it out. I'm humming it to myself because Mile 15 of the Philadelphia Marathon goes right in front of the Philadelphia Museum of Art. Sure, you may not be wearing a gray-on-gray sweatsuit, but you're running where Rocky ran. When you finish back at the museum, feel free to charge up those steps and pound your fists into the air!

■ Just because Patagonia is a sparsely populated region at the ends of the earth does not mean there are no marathoners there. The Patagonian International Marathon—hosted every year in the Magallanes Region of southern Chile, along the Argentinian border—still brings in hundreds of runners. Mile 15 passes alongside the Del Toro Lake, which is named "the bull" because of its often-monstrous swells due to the area's high-powered winds.

■ Toronto has poutine and hockey and BeaverTails, so why not give Canada's most populous city a visit for its annual marathon? At Mile 15, the course passes the CN Tower, an observation tower that was the tallest structure in the world for 32 years. Then it's off to the finish and a half-ton of those maple-flavored cookies to celebrate.

MARATHON VOCAB WORD

BQ: the abbreviation for Boston qualifier, a marathon time that qualifies an individual to run the Boston Marathon

The Boston Marathon, arguably the world's most prestigious, does not have open registration or a lottery like most marathons, and it must be qualified for with a fast time in a previous marathon. For many runners, qualifying for Boston (achieving a BQ) is a lifetime goal. Qualifying times start at three hours for men and three hours and 30 minutes for women, with slower times needed as you get older. Flat courses like Chicago, Berlin, and New Jersey are known for attracting runners in search of a BQ. A word of warning though: due to the increased popularity of marathoning in recent years, achieving a BQ doesn't gain automatic entrance anymore, just the "opportunity to submit for registration."

"If I can run at my current pace until I'm 60, I'll have a BQ. Let's pray I'm a spry old man."

☑ BODY CHECK — The Mind

You're past the halfway mark in this brutal slog of a sporting event, and your body is starting to feel it. Guess who has decided they need to step in? That's right, your brain. Marathon coach Greg McMillan says, "The brain is kind of like a computer. It's monitoring the system, and if it starts to say, 'Wow, these muscle tissues are really getting damaged,' then it is going to cut the power. It's going to send more fatigue messaging. Or, if it's saying, 'We're really running out of fuel, and you're not giving me any fuel, so I'm concerned,' it will make you feel more tired to try to get you to slow down to preserve the system." The mind is a powerful thing that likes to get its way. We've all been on runs where seemingly inexplicably our minds are telling us, "Go home and take a nap."

So how do we tell our brains to shut up? Greg has the answer: "You have to challenge the mind to get used to that type of suffering, so it goes, 'OK. This isn't a threat. This is normal and I can keep going.'" His training tips include fast-finish long runs or progressive runs so you can fatigue the body quickly and then force it to keep running. By putting your brain through a boot camp during those long training runs, you'll make it a much happier organ come Mile 15 of the race. ■

Running with the Motorcade

For anyone who has ever watched a major marathon in person, you know that the elite runners are surrounded on all sides by officials and camera crews. For anyone who has ever watched a major marathon on TV, you know that they've got every angle covered.

Major televised marathons (Boston, New York, the Olympics) have extensive crews, with thousands of pieces of state-of-the-art technology circling around these nearly naked runners as they cruise down city blocks. With separate men's and women's races, these events need two separate crews, and as the pack thins, they need multiple cameras to track the leaders and those running them down. There are trucks with cameras, motorcycles with cameras, helicopters with cameras, and, of course, mounted cameras strategically placed on rooftops along the race. In addition, the leaders are often escorted by police, medical teams, and vehicles full of press and race organizers.

What is it like to run through all the hullabaloo after spending hours training alone? I asked marathon all-stars Shalane Flanagan and Des Linden about their experiences. "Personally, I'm pretty good at just blocking it out," says Des, "and they're far enough removed from us that you're mainly focused on the pack. Their job is to make sure they never get in the way. I know in past races, like with Dick Beardsley, that might be why he lost."

The Dick Beardsley race in question—the 1982 Boston Marathon, where he was narrowly beat by Alberto Salazar—has been dubbed "the duel in the sun" and called one of the greatest marathons ever. In the race's final moments, a hoard of police motorcycles weaved confusingly around the two runners (watch the clips on YouTube to see just how bonkers it was), and when Alberto took the lead, the motorcycles cut off Dick, who had to duck and weave past them in pursuit. Dick lost by just two seconds, leaving many to say that had the police been absent, he might have won.

Nowadays, though, it's mostly just awkward. Shalane recalls an experience during the New York City Marathon: "Paula Radcliffe, the world record holder, was there sitting on the back [of the truck]. She was literally within arm's reach of me, and I could hear her talking about me to the cameraman. So it is kind of awkward when you have friends and acquaintances that you know on the back of those motorcades. You're like, 'Oh, what are they saying about me?'"

"... the second half becomes much more like a training run—just you grinding alone on the road."

Running along with Former *Runner's World* Editor in Chief *Amby Burfoot*

Few people know more about the world of running than Amby Burfoot. His high school cross-country coach was John J. Kelley, 1957 Boston Marathon winner and two-time Olympic marathoner. (He was dubbed "the younger," as there are two famed American marathoners with that name.) He was college roommates with four-time Boston Marathon winner Bill Rodgers. Amby won Boston himself in 1968. Ten years later, he joined *Runner's World*, eventually becoming the magazine's editor in chief. Retired now, Amby still writes regularly for the magazine and has a treasure trove of wisdom about the sport.

You won Boston in 1968. Can you paint a picture for me of what that race looked like?

We were the most motley crew of runners you could possibly imagine. There was no equipment or color or pizzazz. Everyone showed up in gray cotton sweatpants and took them off to run in blue cotton shorts, which were guaranteed to chafe your thighs to bleeding, and a cotton singlet, which would chafe your chest to bleeding. The shoes were so bad we all had bleeding blisters on our feet. There was nothing romantic about it. There was, of course, not a single woman in the field, and the oldest guy was maybe 50 or 55. Nobody could believe that a 55-year-old was still running marathons. There was one reporter from the Boston Globe and a couple photographers, but it was mostly a reunion of 200 or 300 runners in one place. Most of us never saw another runner in our community when we were training. It was our one day a year in the limelight.

MARATHONER

Were there aid stations?

There were no aid stations, and the mile markers numbered the distance backward. There were parents who sliced up oranges and gave them to their kids, who would proffer them to us on the side of the road. Every once in a while, you'd get a lemon instead of an orange.

You've run more than 75 marathons. Is there one that is particularly memorable?

The [Boston Marathon] bombing year, 2013, I was the oldest returning champion. A mile from the finish, we were stopped. I was pissed off that people were stopping us, but as we walked back to the hotel we found out what happened, and then I felt so small and chagrined and stupid for being mad. Everybody thought it was the death of the sport. You could get killed if you ran the Boston Marathon. Well, that lasted about 48 hours, and then we realized that everybody in the world wanted to run the next year to reclaim the streets, to thank the citizens of Boston for all their support through the years. There can never be a marathon that will match Boston 2014 because the energy, the spirit, the rebirth, the celebration, and the reclaiming of the joy of life was so palpable.

How has your body changed over your years of running?

The big change is how much slower you get. I always knew that you got slower as you aged, but through my mid-60s, I was fighting it pretty well. Now in my 70s, I run much slower. I listen to podcasts when I'm running now. I'm going so slow there's no reason I can't concentrate on something else while I'm plodding down the road.

How has marathon culture changed over the years?

The culture has changed because women are running. I happened to run the Marine Corps Marathon with Oprah Winfrey in 1994, and the next spring we had her on the cover of the magazine. It was the best-selling newsstand issue in Runner's World *history, and I think Oprah launched the women's running boom that has continued unabated since the mid-1990s. It's by far the biggest and best change in the sport.*

First Signs of Weakness

There comes a time in every marathon where you feel that first twinge, or notice that nearly imperceptible slowing, or register that slight fogginess in your mind. To any outsider, nothing appears to be the matter, but in your head the first warning light has started blinking. Your body's inevitable breakdown has begun. You may have another two or five or eight good miles left in you, but things are going to get harder.

On bad days, that first sign of weakness might appear earlier. On good days, it might not strike until the final miles, but either way you must accept the coming pain. Shalane Flanagan says, "It's OK to acknowledge you're not going to feel good, but just because that's how you feel doesn't mean that it can't go well. You've got to put your head down and do the work, and hopefully it will turn around. Sometimes it doesn't, and that's OK too."

This realization of coming pain is always frustrating, but that's why we train. If we get used to this feeling of inevitable difficulty, then when it comes we won't say, "I can't do this. It's time to give up." We'll say, "I've done this before, and it was hard, but I got through it. I can push through today, and I'll push through again."

<< *Boston Marathon, Massachusetts, USA, 2004*   **Pages 144–145:** *Jungfrau Marathon, Switzerland, 2011*

Famous Mile 16s

■ The jury is still out as to whether the Loch Ness Monster (or "Nessy" to the sea dragon's close friends) actually exists. The Loch Ness Marathon, however, is 100 percent real, I swear! The point-to-point course traverses the Scottish Highlands, rolling alongside the famed lake for 10 miles, including Mile 16. That's plenty of time for a monster sighting.

■ Mile 16 of the Gettysburg North-South Marathon places runners at the center of the Gettysburg National Military Park. This Pennsylvania marathon commemorates the Civil War's deadliest battle and the turning point for the Union Army in its fight against the Confederacy. Cross the rugged land once commandeered for battlegrounds to honor the soldiers who lost their lives for the freedom of others.

■ While most Canadians speak primarily English, a pocket of the population, predominantly in the province of Québec, speaks a version of French called Québecois. The Québec City Marathon showcases the city's stunning French architecture, including the massive hilltop hotel Le Château Frontenac at Mile 16. Speed through Old Québec as crowds cheer you on in two languages.

MARATHON VOCAB WORD

bandit: someone who runs a marathon illegally, without properly registering or paying to do so

Let's be honest. Marathons can be expensive, and some (for example, New York, Boston, Disney) can be hard to get into, so there is an obvious temptation (especially if you're a local) to just hop the barricade and run. Sure, you might not get the official race time, but you'll have the experience, and if you can print out a fake bib online, you can probably get a medal. Banditing is *highly* controversial in the marathon community. Many are staunchly opposed, as unregistered runners are difficult to treat if injured and steal resources from paying marathoners. Some are fine with it as long as you are conscientious of paying runners and bring your own supplies (and skip the medal). Technically, if your registered friend decides not to run and gives you their bib, you're a bandit, and people are more lenient with that (although let's say you pass out—now they think you're someone who isn't there!). And then there are the true anarchists who just say, "Screw it. You do you."

"Technically, I'm not fast enough to have ever run Boston. Realistically, I've got two medals because I'm a bandit."

✔ BODY CHECK — That First Twinge

We've been going deep on the specifics of the body, so let's zoom back out for a second. You're at Mile 16, and if you've trained well, you've most likely been good up until now. But there comes a point where you feel the first harbinger of pain to come. A small wave of tiredness. A baby ache in the quads. A chafed bit of skin in the armpit. A lack of easily accessible energy, tired muscles, and general fatigue are all stalking you by Mile 16, so if they haven't arrived yet they will soon. If you feel good, be thankful and savor these last moments of clear-minded running joy. If you feel the twinge of pain, brace yourself. It's only going to get worse. ■

Marathon World Records

If you think that the world record for fastest marathon just goes to the person who can run 26.2 miles the fastest, you are wrong. Many of the fastest marathons ever run, including Eliud Kipchoge's dazzling 1:59:40 at the Ineos 1:59 Challenge, do not count. Official world records recognized by World Athletics must be run in an open race where anyone may enter (which excludes Eliud's solo effort). The marathon must also feature a starting line and finish that are not "further apart than 50 percent of the race distance," and it cannot have a substantial decrease in elevation. This eliminates point-to-point courses, like the Boston Marathon, and the mostly downhill mountain courses from eligibility.

For women, there is another level of regulation. If a women's marathon uses male pacers instead of female, then any record is labeled as "mixed sex" and viewed separately from the "women only" record, where female marathon pacers are used.

Here is a quick look at the current marathon world records and how they stack up against individual course records.

World Record
- **MEN: Eliud Kipchoge,** 2:01:39, *Berlin Marathon, 2018*
- **WOMEN (Mixed Sex): Brigid Kosgei,** 2:14:04, *Chicago Marathon, 2019*
- **WOMEN (Women Only): Mary Jepkosgei Keitany,** 2:17:01, *London Marathon, 2017*

Boston Marathon
- **MEN: Geoffrey Mutai,** 2:03:02, *2011*
- **WOMEN: Bizunesh Deba,** 2:19:59, *2014*

New York City Marathon
- **MEN: Geoffrey Mutai,** 2:05:05, *2011*
- **WOMEN: Margaret Okayo,** 2:22:31, *2003*

Women and Men

While the marathon is a painful endeavor for men and women alike, the race has a nasty little way of pinpointing our body's weaknesses. Women and men are each saddled with their own set of obstacles. Here are some physical differences and how they affect running.

☐ **Chest:** This seems like an obvious place to start. Since men don't wear bras, they tend to get bloody nipples from friction with their shirt. Women, however, can incur serious back injuries if they aren't wearing a supportive bra (especially for bigger sizes). Having a large chest can also throw off body posture in general, which can lead to other injuries.

☐ **Thighs:** Women tend to have larger thighs than men, which leads to additional chafing. Men, however, must be careful to wear supportive underwear to protect against an injury between the legs.

☐ **Heart Size:** Men on average have hearts that are 20 percent larger than women. That means they get more blood and thus more oxygen to their extremities, meaning they can run faster and longer on average than women.

☐ **Height:** Men also tend to have longer legs than women, which means they don't take as many steps during the course of a marathon, and thus can finish faster. However, men also carry more weight.

☐ **Weight:** Men tend to be heavier than women, so they are forcing more pounds of pressure on their knees and ankles. Conversely, especially at elite levels where runners are routinely clocking in more than 50 miles a week, female runners can face issues in not weighing enough. Excessive exercise and low body fat can throw off hormone levels in the body and lead to amenorrhea (missed periods). So no matter your weight, it's always important to consult a doctor before taking up marathoning.

☐ **Hormones:** Men have testosterone and women have estrogen. Testosterone helps increase muscles, while estrogen accumulates more fat, meaning that men tend to be stronger and thus able to run faster.

☐ **Iron:** Women's bodies need more iron than men's do, in part due to women's periods. Elyse Kopecky says that, in general, "Women's systems can be more complex with hormones and fluctuation throughout the month. Their needs vary, while men's needs are more consistent." She urges women to be aware of their cravings, as they're often for nutrients the body is running low on.

☐ **Fat:** Women carry more fat on their bodies than men and also need more fat in their diet. Elyse says, "The demands of running can really call for a lot more fat in the diet. When I'm in serious training, I'm eating an avocado every single day, and I really focus on good healthy sauces with every meal to get in the good healthy fats." (I'm choosing to count ranch dressing as a "healthy sauce.")

☐ **Bones:** Due to their smaller bodies, women tend to have smaller, thinner bones than men. Especially in older women, these bones may become increasingly fragile due to a lack of estrogen or developing osteoporosis. While this can't always be treated, adding vitamin C into your diet can decrease your risk of stress fractures and other bone injuries.

☐ **Armpits:** Physically armpits of men and women are not that different, but women often shave their armpits while men don't. Armpit stubble, however, can create a hell of a chafe, so male or female, if you're going to shave the pits, keep them nice and smooth on race day.

The Olympic Marathon's 100th Birthday

The 100-year anniversary of the modern Olympics was held not in Athens, but in Atlanta, Georgia, a place nearly as hot, hilly, and humid as the Greek original. This time women were allowed, though it was just their fourth shot at the marathon (the first was in 1984). When the race morning dawned a bit overcast, Fatuma Roba, from the cool mountainous region of Ethiopia's capital, was pleased. She'd slogged through her first marathon just two years before: "When I finished, I said, 'Never again will I do this distance. It is too long!'" (Paging champs Grete Waitz and Meb Keflezighi, who both said the same!) She had to be hospitalized after her second marathon. But at the Olympics, Roba was all in. She took the lead around Mile 11 and never wavered, finishing in 2:26:05, beating the field by a full two minutes to become the first African woman to win gold in the Olympic Marathon and herald the rise of African women in the sport. Roba also went on to win Boston three years in a row, beginning in 1997.

▪ ▪ ▪ ▪
Running along with Runner-of-all-Trades *Danielle Quatrochi*

Danielle Quatrochi is the president and chief operating officer at Pocket Outdoor Media. That's the endurance sports publisher behind magazines like *Women's Running* and *Triathlete*, so clearly she knows a thing or two about running. She has also worked in the world of sports retail for brands like Finish Line, Nike, and Adidas.

Oh, and she just so happened to qualify for the 2012 Olympic Trials in the marathon (no easy task) with a time of 2:44:56. And that was while working full time *and* raising two daughters! Danielle has worked on all sides of the sport, so I picked her brain on all kinds of running-related topics.

What makes the marathon such a special event?
I love that marathons support all levels of runners. There is no gender, age, race, or ability that discriminates the opportunity to participate. It's an amazing reason to travel and see a city or place that you wouldn't be able to see in a car. It's a celebration of hard work and achievement.

In working for Pocket Outdoor Media and its brands, have you noticed any trends in running or the marathon?
The footwear-technology landscape has changed so much over the years, from the focus of running shoes that gave you stability to shoes that let your foot move more naturally and freely to create stronger feet and avoid injury. There isn't one technology or training that is a one-size-fits-all approach, so it's about providing guidance that is personalized to fit a specific runner's needs. It's a lot more complex for brands to connect with runners today. They have to pay more attention to the insights and build products and marketing that is more personalized than ever.

Why do you think the marathon is so popular now as opposed to, say, 40 years ago?

I find that the everyday runner isn't only inspired by elite athletes. They also look for inspiring stories of everyday people doing extraordinary things. This makes running feel more accessible, and people can better picture themselves trying the sport.

Are there differences in how journalists cover the marathon as opposed to other sports?

There are so many life stories to share behind the marathon. It's not just about the results or the records broken. It's so much more about the journey of getting to the starting line. I don't believe there are too many sports where you train for months for just one event.

As a businesswoman and a mother, how do you still find time to run these long marathon distances?

I do juggle a lot, but one thing that helps me manage the stress of life is running. I prefer to run in the morning, so I can better handle anything that comes up during the day. I also try to run with girlfriends who offer their support in both running and life. I don't look at running as just an exercise or a need to get faster; it's so much more than that. It's daily therapy, a reason to get outside, and a reason to connect with friends. It's something I hope my children get to experience one day, and if I lead my lifestyle through running, then they too may appreciate it.

MILE 17

The Wandering Mind

As we trudge through the back half of the marathon, the mind becomes an increasingly potent force. Early in the race, you're all high spirits and nervous energy. You're dialed into your best race, your goals, and the dream of crossing that finish line like a champion. By Mile 17, though, your mind may be proceeding down one of two long, tremulous hallways.

Problem number one is a mind fixated on suffering. Once your mind latches onto that pain in your calf or how fatigued your muscles are, it can be hard to distract it away from its mission of getting you to quit running. Faced with this challenge, runners employ all manner of mental gymnastics to distract it. Lindsay Crouse says, "I do a lot of math when I race. It's a good distraction because I'm not very good at math, division in particular." Sometimes I'll give myself the order of listing off every teacher I had in high school as a diversion.

This, however, brings us to problem number two: a mind not focused on the race. If you're running for a PR or a BQ, you don't want a wandering mind because that means you're probably slowing down without even realizing it. Shalane Flanagan says, "The days I'm struggling and not feeling good, I'm drifting to other thoughts. I'll calculate how much longer until I get to the finish line, think about what I'm going to eat. I'm trying to distract myself and not focusing on what I'm doing in that moment."

So, yeah, throw "unfocused mind" on the ever-growing pile of obstacles you're facing as you run a marathon.

<< Dubai Marathon, United Arab Emirates, 2015

Famous Mile 17s

■ The Twin Cities Marathon lives up to its name, exploring both Minneapolis and St. Paul. And there, separating Minnesota's two largest cities, runs the Mississippi River. The river also divides the two halves of the marathon, as runners circle Minneapolis before racing along the longest river in the United States for several miles, including Mile 17. Then it's off to the other twin, St. Paul, and the finish.

■ If you're tired of cushy street marathons, give yourself a challenge with the Equinox Marathon held every year in Fairbanks, Alaska. The elevation gain is more than 3,000 feet, and nearly the entire race is run on trails and dirt roads in the backwoods of the state. The race is also run in September (i.e., in the cold). As a reward, though, Mile 17 runs along the Ester Dome, which gives runners a breathtaking view of Denali (on a clear day).

■ Washington, DC's Marine Corps Marathon is an embarrassment of riches when it comes to notable landmarks, and nowhere is that clearer than Mile 17. Marathoners begin the mile passing the famed Lincoln Memorial, a boon for any race. Before the mile is over, however, runners also trot beside the Reflecting Pool, the World War II Memorial, and the Washington Monument. And that's just in one mile, folks.

✔ BODY CHECK — Running vs. Walking

"Walking is powerful," says marathoner Dr. Mark Cucuzzella. Even if you're not using the run-walk-run method of marathoning from the jump, slowing down for a bit in a race (say, Mile 17?) can be advantageous. Whether due to fatigue or breathing issues or cramping, many runners slow dramatically at some point in the second half of the marathon. Rather than trudge along in a plodding agony, Mark suggests that walking can serve as a nice reset. It gets your heart rate down, resets your breathing, and allows you to regain good posture. Then you can tackle the second half of the marathon with much more vigor. Sometimes slowing down in the short term can help you speed up in the long term. ■

run-walk:

a method of long-distance running that intercuts running with short stints of walking to lower the overall race time

It may seem counterintuitive to the "just keep running" model of marathoning most runners employ, but there are many marathoners who achieve faster times by mixing running and walking. The general idea is that your muscles get very tired out with straight running for four hours. If you give them some time to breathe, however, they'll be fresher longer and you can ultimately trim time off your PR. The run-walk or run-walk-run method is also a great strategy for more injury-prone runners. It puts less consistent stress on your knees and ankles, allows for some recovery during the race, and reduces your body temperature. One downside of the run-walk method, however, is that you need to do a good bit of math as well as keep meticulous timing during the race.

"I spent two hours on Saturday determining my run-walk split times, so now I'm good to go for this marathon!"

"Sometimes slowing down in the short term can help you speed up in the long term."

Running along with Joggler *Michal Kapral*

No, I didn't misspell the word *jogger*. Michal Kapral, while a runner, is also the world's fastest marathon *joggler*, a portmanteau of the words *jogger* and *juggler*. Yes, that's right, Michal runs full marathons while juggling. In 2007, he joggled 26.2 miles in 2:50:12, a time most marathoners could only dream about sans three balls. In 2016, he ran the Chicago Marathon without dropping a single ball. That, my friends, is talent. Naturally I had a lot of questions for Michal, which he kindly answered.

Before you started joggling, you actually broke the world record for fastest running of a marathon while pushing a stroller. How did that come about?

My sister Moira and I used to flip through the Guinness World Records *book looking for records that we could maybe beat, and I saw records about the marathon. After winning the Toronto Marathon, I was looking for things to do next, and I saw the stroller record.*

And then you announced that you were going to joggle the marathon the following year without even knowing how to juggle. How did that idea come to you?

I hadn't actually been thinking about it, but it was one of the records I had read in the book, and I was like, "Whoa, fastest marathon joggling! That sounds amazing!" I just thought, "Let's go for it!"

How did you prepare for your first joggling marathon?

I started with juggling balls I ordered online. They looked really cool, but they were quite heavy and much harder to juggle than the beanbags I use now. I didn't really know what I was doing, so just as the sun was coming up, I would go to the local park trail system and start learning how to joggle. I dropped the balls literally every three seconds. It was hilarious. I almost quit many, many times just because it was such a sorry scene. I was alone in the semidarkness, trying to run and juggle. The balls would fall on the ground, and those first ones were slick, so they'd fall and roll into a ditch or a muddy puddle. My arms were killing me, too, because I had poor technique. But it's amazing what you can do when you just keep at it. Eventually I got to the point where I was hardly dropping at all.

What is it about joggling that made you keep doing it after that race?

There's nothing else quite like it in giving you a hand-eye coordination and upper and lower body endurance workout all together. Maybe cross-country skiing is the closest thing, but you don't quite get the beauty of having this juggling pattern floating in front of you as you're also trying to run fast. There's something really poetic about it. It combines a little bit of circus with flat-out endurance. I find the juggling pattern gets you in a zen mode at the beginning of the marathon. You need to control the pattern in front of you with the pace you're running and your arm swing. When it all works together and clicks, it's really something beautiful.

What are some of the difficulties in joggling besides, of course, juggling while running?

I have had several joggling-related injuries. The first marathon, I got this massive lump growing out of the side of my wrist that was very painful. A couple years ago, I torqued this muscle in my upper shoulder big time, and I went to a physiotherapist. She was laughing her head off, saying this is the first juggling-related injury she'd had to treat.

Can you tell me a little about the joggling community?

When I ran my first joggling marathon, I thought I was the only one, and then, all of a sudden, all these other jogglers came out of the woodwork and got in touch with me. I just keep hearing from more and more people all over the world—pretty much on every continent—and we share this unique passion. It's a pretty tight-knit community that I did not expect. Joggling is surprisingly addictive. I thought I would only do it once, but I miss it when I'm running and not juggling, so I try to do it as much as possible just because it's fun.

MILE 18

The Second Wind

Don't get me wrong. The second half of the marathon isn't all bad. Hell, some of you are probably still feeling great at Mile 18, and others may have caught their second wind. There is the initial, and often devastating, realization that you will not feel carefree and speedy the entire marathon (because for some reason I go into every race thinking maybe this time it will be easy the whole way). After this realization sinks in, however, you will acclimate to the new normal.

Sure, your body is not as fresh as it was at Mile 4, but you are still trotting along at a nice clip. Somehow these miles of "not great but still good" running are usually my favorite because they feel so precious. Mile 2 is almost always going to be a breeze, but when you get a manageable Mile 20, now that is a gift.

Spend some time during this brief reprieve to admire your surroundings. So much of the back half of the course is focused on your crumbling body that you don't notice what's around you. Give a high five to a cheering kid. Encourage another runner who is worse off than yourself. Smile at a volunteer without grimacing. In the marathon, you have to take the tiny joys where you can.

<< *Mumbai Marathon, India, 2011*

Famous Mile 18s

■ If you like looking at mountains without climbing them, the Kilimanjaro Marathon might be your speed. The race, run annually in Tanzania, takes runners near the base of Africa's tallest peak at Mile 18 without forcing them to scale it. As a bonus, some of the aid stations dole out Coca-Cola along with the standard water.

■ Why not add a marathon to your Tahitian getaway? The Moorea Marathon, run on Tahiti's sister French Polynesian island, has a nearly 100 percent beachfront route. Enjoy views of sandbars and endless ocean as you trace the northern coast of the Pacific paradise. Mile 18 runs along the volcanic island's Cook's Bay.

■ And while we're talking about mountains and bodies of water, there is also a marathon run annually around the rim of Oregon's Crater Lake National Park. The lake, formed when a volcano collapsed and sourced completely from rain and melting snow, can be seen from the majority of the course, including Mile 18. As an aside, the race starts near a rock formation in the lake called Wizard Island, so that's pretty cool.

BODY CHECK — Hot Spots and Blisters

If you are at Mile 18 of the marathon and you get a blister, what can you do? The depressing answer is not much. Your last *eight miles* are just going to suck. So, ladies and gents, we need to stave off those dreaded blisters (and their nasty little precursor, the hot spot) long before the marathon. Blisters (usually on a runner's foot) are caused by prolonged friction between skin and the shoe or sock. These are especially common (and virtually unavoidable) for new runners, but your skin will eventually thicken up. There are two things to avoid. First, don't get an infected blister. When you get blisters while training, make sure to keep them clean so they will heal and turn into callouses. Second, don't switch up your gear at the last minute. Your feet will toughen up where they need to during your training, but a change in socks or shoes can start creating friction in tender new areas. If you need new shoes, get them at the beginning of a training cycle. ■

runhole:

a person who is so obsessed with running that they annoy or neglect their friends

A portmanteau of *runner* and *asshole*, *runhole* is a generally endearing name that friends and family use to poke fun at their running-fanatic loved ones. Runholes may engage in any of the following activities: running often and for long distances; constantly talking about their runs, their races, their gear, their times, and anything else tangentially related to running; frequently posting about running on social media; wearing running- or race-related clothing; skipping events to run; casually dropping their marathons into casual conversation in a very casual, non-bragging way, and casually waiting for people to be impressed with them; wearing race medals to non-running-related events (like Thanksgiving) just to remind their family that they are, in fact, the most athletic sibling; screaming in their quiet office on a Tuesday when they learn they won the New York City Marathon lottery; and ordering dessert because "they ran 23 miles before brunch."

"Matthew is such a runhole. He showed up to a baptism wearing a foil blanket."

Con Woman on the Course

Rosie Ruiz wowed crowds at the 1980 Boston Marathon by clocking a women's Boston record of 2:31:56, becoming the third-fastest women's marathon winner ever. But not so fast (ha). Not only was Ruiz remarkably unsweaty, she'd also bested her qualifying New York City Marathon time by 25 minutes! That was especially amazing because she'd been allowed to register late for New York due to a professed brain tumor. When Boston men's winner Bill Rodgers asked Ruiz about her splits, unlike every other runner in the world, she couldn't remember them. No one could remember seeing her on the course in Boston or New York either. But someone did recall seeing her on the New York subway— during the marathon—and in Boston, two Harvard students spotted her standing in the crowd a half mile from the finish. It didn't take long before Ruiz was declared the world's most famous course cutter. The real women's winner was Canadian Jacqueline Gareau, whose 2:34:28 was indeed a true course record.

MILE 19 Pop Culture

While we're in our brief respite from hardship, let's talk about the marathon out in the real world. Most people (sadly) will never run a marathon, many will never even watch one, but just about everyone knows that it is a *looooooooooooooong* running race. (If I had a dollar for every time someone asked, "Well, how long is this one?"—insinuating that marathons come in different lengths—I'd be able to afford at least one fancy dinner.)

Outside of running circles, the marathon is perceived as a crowning achievement that few elite-level athletes can accomplish. When I was growing up, there was one man in our town who ran marathons, and we all knew him by that distinguishing factor. While more people are running marathons (and certainly halves) these days, most people still have only a vague understanding of the sport, culled from the Olympics, an episode of *The Simpsons*, or their sister's one ex-boyfriend who was always running.

While that means that many people who could run a marathon will never feel the sense of accomplishment that comes from running 26.2, it also means that, when you cross that finish line, you've joined an elite and mysterious club placed on a pedestal by society. So, as you run Mile 19, envision yourself in the office on Monday with your medal, your coworkers in awe that you ran "like 50 miles or something."

<< New York City Marathon, New York, USA, 2017

streaker: someone who has finished the same marathon multiple years in a row

Get your mind out of the gutter! Nude activists sprinting across the Super Bowl field aren't the only kind of streaker. It's also a term given to the men and women who run the same races year after year. While it may seem masochistic, many runners return to the same marathons annually as a tradition. Running the same marathon year after year lets you watch the course and event evolve, and teaches you the best way to run that marathon. Plus, many marathons offer perks to streakers, so you might want to sign up for your local marathon again next year.

"Gerry is a Detroit Marathon streaker. He has run it every year since he was 22!"

Famous Mile 19s

■ Remember how the Marine Corps Marathon is stockpiled with sights to see? Well, here we are just two miles later running past the US Capitol. Oprah was on to something when she picked to run this marathon back in 1994 (with a time of 4:29, no less).

■ After passing the Louvre, the Bastille, the Château de Vincennes, Notre Dame Cathedral, *and* the Seine River, the Paris Marathon finally arrives at the Eiffel Tower during Mile 19. The 26.2 in the City of Lights is another race with few dead zones. Between the massive crowds and spectacular roadside attractions, the miles melt away without you even noticing.

■ When the winner of a marathon struggles to break three hours, you know the race is a beast. The Jungfrau Marathon, run annually in the Alps outside of Interlaken, Switzerland, is one such slow, painful (but beautiful) endeavor. The incredibly steep marathon features a short reprieve from the climbing around Mile 19 in the town of Wengen before another half-dozen miles of ascent. Bagpipers serenade the highest point of the race, though, so there's that to look forward to.

BODY CHECK—Dizziness

We're 19 miles in, which means more extreme problems are on their way for some runners. One such issue is dizziness, and, if it's not handled well, fainting. Some of the most common causes are dehydration, low blood sugar, and overexertion. Basically, if you're not drinking enough, if you haven't eaten enough carbs, or if your body overheats, you could start to feel dizzy. While you can push through dizziness for a mile or so, if it happens early, it's best to address the issue. Get that fueling you need or cool off. Another strange cause of dizziness is actually stopping. If you get tired and stop at an aid station after 19 miles of pumping away, your blood pressure could drop suddenly, resulting in lightheadedness or, in extreme cases, fainting. Whenever you stop running, try to keep walking so your blood pressure has time to recalibrate. We've entered the danger zone, folks, so keep a close eye on how you're feeling. ■

Run for Charity

If you need a little extra motivation to run 26.2, why not run for a charity? Many marathons give runners the option of raising a specific amount of money for an array of charities in exchange for entrance to the race. Jim Heim, the New York City Marathon's race director, says, "Our charity program is enormous. Every year we raise about $40 million, with 10,000 of the runners running directly for charity." That's an astronomical amount of money, mostly raised in bits and pieces by runners from around the world.

So why do runners choose this method of entry? The most cynical answer is that they can't get in any other way. Some races, like New York City, use a lottery to pick runners since so many people are desperate to get in. If you lose the lottery, you can still run if you're willing to raise several thousand dollars for a charity. Just pick your charity on the website, send the donation link to everyone you know, and, once you've hit the required amount, you're in the race! Other races, like Boston, have a time threshold, so if you're not fast enough but still want to run the historic race, you can sign up for a charity slot.

More importantly, though, running for charity makes your marathon extra meaningful. You're more likely to train and run the race if you know you're putting yourself through the agony for more than just yourself. Similarly, during the race, knowing you're running for someone else can give you that extra boost. Many charities station teams to cheer along the course, and no one screams louder than those fans when they see someone with their charity's shirt coming around the corner.

So, if you're looking for a spot in a sold-out marathon, a little extra motivation, or just a way to give back, give running for charity a try.

Marathons on Screens Big and Small

Cheers. Tears. The thrill of competition. Overcoming adversity. Waddling into a sweaty port-o-john at Mile 19 only to find someone else has pooed on the seat. Marathons have everything a filmmaker dreams of, so naturally a few movies (and TV episodes) have been dedicated to the sport. Here are some of the most iconic.

☐ **Brittany Runs a Marathon (2019):** Based on a true story, Brittany (played by Jillian Bell) tries to get her unsatisfying life back on track by signing up for the New York City Marathon. Scenes from the movie were actually shot during the 2017 race, so those extras are real runners exhibiting *real pain*.

☐ **Stronger (2017):** The Boston Marathon bombing has inspired several movies, but Jake Gyllenhaal's portrayal of Jeff Bauman, who lost both of his legs while cheering for his girlfriend at the finish line, is especially gripping.

☐ **Rizzoli & Isles, "Born to Run" (2010):** A *classic* marathon narrative. Two friends start the race. At Mile 3, they discover a dead body. By the marathon's end, they've solved the murder. We've all been there.

☐ **Der Räuber (2010):** This little-known German movie is loosely based on the life of Johann Kastenberger, who ran marathons, killed people, and robbed banks wearing a Ronald Reagan mask. Now tell me you don't want to watch this film.

☐ **Run, Fat Boy, Run (2007):** If you can beat your ex-fiancée's new fiancé in a marathon, maybe she'll take you back. Such is Simon Pegg's thinking in this British rom-com. To be fair, I would also gladly run 26.2 miles to try and win Thandie Newton's heart.

☐ **Seinfeld, "The Hot Tub" (1995):** Elaine has a runner staying at her house for the New York City Marathon and Jerry is obsessed with making sure he gets to the race on time. After numerous mishaps he makes it to the race . . . only to be scalded by some hot tea from Kramer that he mistakes for a water cup.

☐ **Forrest Gump (1994):** Run, Forrest, run! When Tom Hanks's titular character gets his heart broken by Jenny, he decides to run (very relatable). Less relatable is not stopping for three years.

☐ **Sesame Street, "Episode 1836" (1983):** Snuffleupagus decides to run the New York City Marathon and Big Bird is there to cheer him on. Snuffy shows up to the race late, stops at stop signs on the racecourse, and finishes dead last. But when he crosses the line in the middle of the night, Big Bird is still there to congratulate him. This is undoubtedly the sweetest marathon story ever told.

☐ **Marathon Man (1976):** Running marathons has many upsides, but not until watching this Dustin Hoffman thriller would I have guessed that being able to outrun bad guys after escaping from an evil dentist with a drill was one of them. It's not really about marathons, but Dustin's character, Babe, is a marathon runner.

Famous Marathoners and Their Times

The marathon is a sport for everyone, and everyone includes celebrities! They often tackle the marathon to raise money and awareness for charities. Here is a quick rundown of the rich and famous who have pounded the pavement for 26.2 miles, sorted by their finishing times. Where do you slot in?

Celebrity	Time	Marathon	Year
Dana Carvey (actor)	3:04:21	Ocean to Bay	1972
Bryan Cranston (actor)	3:20:45	New York City	1985
Apolo Ohno (speedskater)	3:25:12	New York City	2011
Gordon Ramsay (chef)	3:30:37	London	2004
George W. Bush (president)	3:44:52	Houston	1993
Christy Turlington Burns (model)	3:46:35	London	2015
Edward Norton (actor)	3:48:01	New York City	2009
Ryan Reynolds (actor)	3:50:22	New York City	2008
Natalie Dormer (actress)	3:50:57	London	2014
Kerri Strug (gymnast)	3:56:06	New York City	2011
Will Ferrell (actor)	3:56:12	Boston	2003
Sarah Palin (politician)	3:59:36	Humpy's Classic	2005
Bobby Flay (chef)	4:01:37	New York City	2010
Sean Astin (actor)	4:04:00	Los Angeles	2012
Kevin Hart (comedian/actor)	4:05:06	New York City	2017
Jennie Finch (softball player)	4:05:26	New York City	2011
Sean Combs (rapper)	4:14:54	New York City	2003
Alanis Morissette (musician)	4:17:03	Bizz Johnson Trail	2009
Mario Lopez (actor/host)	4:23:29	New York City	2011
Ethan Hawke (actor)	4:25:30	New York City	2015
Tiki Barber (football player)	4:28:26	New York City	2016
Oprah Winfrey (host/actress)	4:29:15	Marine Corps	1994
Shia LaBeouf (actor)	4:35:31	Los Angeles	2010
Drew Carey (comedian)	4:37:11	Marine Corps	2011
Karlie Kloss (model)	4:41:49	New York City	2017
Al Gore (vice president)	4:58:25	Marine Corps	1997
Valerie Bertinelli (actress)	5:14:37	Boston	2010
Chip Gaines (TV host)	5:21:54	Waco	2018
Katie Holmes (actress)	5:29:58	New York City	2007
Pamela Anderson (model/actress)	5:41:03	New York City	2013
Alicia Keys (musician)	5:50:52	New York City	2015
Carole Radziwill (reality TV star)	6:42:06	New York City	2017
Al Roker (weatherman)	7:09:44	New York City	2010

Running along with Streakers *Bennett Beach and Dave Obelkevich*

For most people, one marathon is too much. One a year for the rest of your life? Unthinkable. And yet that is exactly what Bennett Beach and Dave Obelkevich, both in their 70s, have done. The two men claim the longest streaks for two of America's most prestigious marathons. As of 2019, Dave has completed 44 New York City Marathons in a row, while Bennett has soldiered through a staggering 52 Boston Marathons, just a few shy of marathon legend Johnny Kelley's 58 Boston finishes. I chatted with both men about their impressive streaks and how the marathon has changed over their long tenures.

Can you tell me how you decided to run your first marathon?

Bennett: *Spring of my senior year of high school, I just happened to be listening to the radio and heard the Boston Marathon. It was sleeting, a terrible day, and just the craziness of it really appealed to me. I was going to be in Boston the next year for college, and I thought, "I'm going to run it." At that point, the longest I'd ever run was maybe five miles. I was so unprepared for that race. I trained by adding a mile every day in the weeks leading up to the race [not a good strategy], and I ate steak the morning of the race.*

Dave: *It was in 1972, and I was watching a news program the day after the New York City Marathon. Until 1976, the race was four loops of Central Park, and I told my wife, "If they can do four loops, I can do one." The next year, I waited on the west side of Central Park, and when the runners came, I joined. I ran one loop in 43 minutes, and I had so much fun. I said, "Wow, I'm going to get a number next year." I ran it in 1974 and I never felt worse after a race than that.*

When did you decide to be a streaker?

Bennett: *I didn't really think about it. I thought, "I'm going to do this as long as I can because it's satisfying and fun."*

⌃ *Bennett Beach*

⌃ Dave Obelkevich

Dave: *It never occurred to me not to do it because I always knew dozens of people from my running club who were doing it. It wasn't until 10 or 15 years ago that the New York Road Runners called and told me I had a streak going.*

Was there a year you almost didn't run and broke your streak?
Bennett: *The fourth one I almost didn't finish. I had a knee problem, and a few miles in I felt bad so I asked a cop where the loser's bus was. He said he didn't see it, so I thought I'd just keep running until it caught up. After a while my knee numbed up, and I finished.*
Dave: *I often procrastinate things, and one year I was rejected for signing up too late. My wife told me to write a letter to the race director, Fred Lebow. In late August, she asked if I wrote the letter, and I said, "No." She said, "Well, then I'll write a letter." I got in, so it's because of her that I have the streak.*

Are there any perks to being the longest streaker of your marathon?
Bennett: *It peaked in 2017, when I ran number 50. The Boston Athletic Association was really kind to me and showed me a lot of attention. I got to throw out the first ball at a Red Sox game that year, which was a real kick.*

How many marathons have you run total?
Bennett: *80.*
Dave: *112 marathons and 200 ultramarathons, so more ultras than regular marathons.*

How has the marathon changed over the years?
Bennett: *In those first years, it was just men. We'd all be changing clothes in the middle school gymnasium before the start. There'd be a doctor up in the bleachers with a stethoscope confirming that we were healthy enough to run, and the whole place reeked of Bengay. After the race, we'd all go into the Prudential Building. There were showers, and they'd be serving up beef stew.*

"... when you cross that finish line you've joined an elite and mysterious club placed on a pedestal by society."

Dave: *There are a lot more women now. The first few years of New York, I think a total of five or six women finished. Another difference is that there are a lot of older people. The first three years of the marathon, the oldest finisher was 52, and I'm 76 now. Also, the average runner is a lot slower, and there are a lot more runners coming in from other countries, which is wonderful for the city.*

What is your favorite marathon memory?

Bennett: *Finishing my first marathon is one of the great moments of my life. I'm 70, and it still ranks up there. I finished in 3:23 and was ecstatic. Coming down that final line at Boylston and hearing my name announced, thousands of people cheering—it was mind-blowing.*

Dave: *The first one. You can only finish your first marathon once. It is going to be a very special day.*

Hitting the Wall

And just like that you hit it: the dreaded wall. It wasn't there until it was, and now you are *feeling* this race. You were cruising along with minimal discomfort, and now you feel like the girl in a horror movie who has just jumped through a third-floor glass window, landed on the back patio, and is stumbling down the driveway in a terrified, pain-addled haze. You've come this far, so you can't quit, but your body sure does want to and going fast is no longer an option. You are slowing down, like *way* down. Like that-group-of-people-walking-to-brunch-on-the-sidewalk-just-passed-me slow.

Once you've hit the wall, there's really no easy fix. Des Linden says, "The big thing is just reminding yourself why you got into this, why you're doing it." While you're at your low points (and don't you worry, you can get lower), remember all of the reasons why you're running this race and imagine just how good it will feel to cross that finish line. It will be all the sweeter because of the pain you're enduring now.

Famous Mile 20s

■ Sure, the New York City Marathon gets all the attention, but its plucky neighbor race, the New Jersey Marathon, has plenty to offer. It's flatter, faster, and comes with plenty of ocean views. Mile 20 steers runners onto the Asbury Park Boardwalk, past Bruce Springsteen's old haunt, The Stone Pony, and through the abandoned Beaux-Arts Asbury Park Casino and Carousel House. Don't sleep on New Jersey.

■ It will be a surprise to no one that Mile 20 of the Bahamas Marathon is run alongside a beach, specifically on the northern coast of Nassau. If you like the Caribbean and are looking for some extra bling, you can sign up for the Five Island Challenge, which doles out an impressive finisher medal for those who complete marathons in Bermuda, Jamaica, Barbados, the Cayman Islands, and the Bahamas.

■ In the northeastern corner of Georgia, just south of Chattanooga, Tennessee, the Union and Confederate forces squared off against one another back in 1863. Today, the Chickamauga Battlefield Marathon runs to commemorate those lost in the Civil War, with Mile 20 marking the turning point in the race's second loop of the park. Consider it for your first marathon—if you're a rookie, they'll give you a framed copy of your bib.

MARATHON VOCAB WORD

hitting the wall: the sudden fatigue that overcomes runners near the end of a marathon

As you're pounding through 26.2 miles, your body is obviously using energy. Duh. But there are different kinds of energy stored in your body, and some are more easily accessible than others. The most readily available is glycogen, a carbohydrate stored in your liver and muscles. The reason runners carb-load is to maximize their glycogen stash. Unfortunately, most bodies only store around 2,000 calories of glycogen, so as you hit Miles 18 to 22, you are running on empty (most runners burn 100 calories per mile). Now your body must switch over to fat, which is harder to access (that's why losing weight is so hard!). It's this transition that makes you very tired all of a sudden. If this transition is the issue, there are two ways of softening the blow. The first is to supply your body with more carbs and glycogen during the race by eating gels or other energy sources. This, however, can cause stomach issues if you overdo it. The other technique is to get your body used to running off fat by training with long-distance runs where your body must access the fat storage. Neither method is foolproof though. A third option, of course, is to take a break during Mile 13 for a baguette.

"Man! I hit the wall around Mile 20 and just wanted to collapse on someone's lawn."

✔ BODY CHECK — The Wall

OK, so I know at the beginning of this chapter I wrote about how "the wall" is "hit" because of glycogen storage and whatnot. This is true. But "the wall" is also a nebulous phrase that runners apply to just about any large obstacle they collide with during the marathon's last 10 miles. Marathon coach Greg McMillan describes it as "a massive slowing of pace. People will slow down not just 10 seconds per mile, but one, two, three, or four minutes per mile." So yes, low glycogen stores are a culprit, but they're far from the only one. Muscle fatigue is another, especially if you haven't trained hard. Three hours' worth of pounding on muscles can leave them torn and sore. The mind is also trying to slow you down to preserve the body. Tiredness and cramps are two common methods there. Another cause of the wall is gastrointestinal issues. As the GI system dehydrates, gels and sports drinks you've taken in can cause disruption in the stomach. Cue vomiting or diarrhea, which in turn brings about more dehydration. All this to say, the wall is a many-headed Scylla lurking in the back half of the marathon. There's no surefire way to avoid it, but planning ahead can go a long way to subduing the beast. ■

Break Up with Your Marathon Buddy?

You're at Mile 20. You're feeling strong. You want that PR. But running beside you is your husband or girlfriend or mom or best friend, and they are struggling. They'll make it 26.2, God willing, but it is going to be a slog. The million-dollar question: Do you ditch them?

If you're running with someone (even someone you've trained with), this scenario can (and most likely will) rear its head in the back half of the marathon. You never know how your body is going to react on race day, so it's best to be prepared. Chat up your running buddies before the race starts and feel out the situation. Do you want to finish together no matter what? Are you both OK splitting up? Does one of you care more about time than the other? You don't want to leave your boyfriend staggering on the side of the road and create eternal resentment if you can help it.

"While you're at your low points, remember all of the reasons why you're running this race and imagine just how good it will feel to cross that finish line."

Des Linden's Book Club

Boston Marathon winner Des Linden is passionate about many things: coffee, whiskey, running (obviously), and reading! Don't believe me? Just check out her Instagram. Here are three of her favorite books on running.

☐ *Once a Runner* by John L. Parker Jr.: Few sports novels are more beloved than this one, which focuses on a college runner trying to break the four-minute mile barrier in the shadow of the Vietnam War. "He writes running really well," says Des. "You're like, 'Oh yeah, this is just like me!'"

☐ *Running with the Buffaloes* by Chris Lear: "It's kind of a nerd runner book," Des says of this narrative, which follows the University of Colorado men's cross-country team during its 1998 season. Inspirational and informative, it's perfect for anyone intrigued by what it takes to be a great runner.

☐ *Let Your Mind Run* by Deena Kastor: You can't talk about modern marathoning in the United States without mentioning Olympic medalist Deena Kastor (who has run side by side with Des on multiple occasions). Her 2018 memoir follows her storied career, focusing on the mental strength needed to compete in marathons.

MILE 21 — Regret

In my humble opinion, Mile 21 is the worst mile of the marathon. By this point, the average runner has been slogging away for more than three hours. You are *exhausted*, and despite all this pain, you still have five more miles to run. That's close to an hour's worth, especially if you're rapidly slowing down, and a lot of us are.

Welcome fellow travelers to the land of regret! It's around this point that you'll start questioning why you ever made the horrifically ill-conceived choice to enter a marathon. Cheryl in legal ran one and said it was empowering, but what does she know? This is not empowering. This is the bowels of human misery, and you've always hated Cheryl anyway. Curses on her and her entire extended family. The marathon is clearly a race orchestrated by the devil, Judas, and Adolf Hitler.

It's Mile 21, where you will solemnly promise to yourself that if you finish the marathon (a big "if "considering your body feels like it has been run over by an industrial-grade lawn mower) you will never run another step in your life voluntarily. Sure, you said the same thing the last 15 marathons you ran, but this time is different. This time you're going to remember this pain, and no matter how good crossing that finish line feels, you're going to stick to your guns. This is your retirement, and from now on the only marathons for you are Netflix binges of *Schitt's Creek*. Yep. This is the last one. Definitely . . .

<< *Boston Marathon, Massachusetts, USA, 2006*

leapfrogging: to repeatedly pass and be passed by the same runner

In a typical marathon, you are running with so many people that none of them stick out in your brain (aside from the guy dressed up like a banana, of course), but, especially if you're having a rough go in the back half, you may start to see the same people over and over. You get tired and they pass you. You get a burst of energy and you pass them. They pass you again, and then you pass them. Leapfrogging can be discouraging, but use it as a distraction from the pain and a motivation to keep going. In the 2018 Walt Disney World Marathon, I was leapfrogging with a woman dressed as Tinker Bell, and I credit her for making sure I never stopped to walk.

"After the guy with the man bun leapfrogged me for the third time, I decided my only goal was to finish before him."

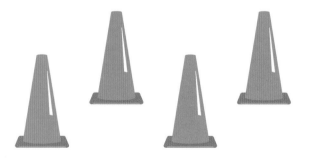

Famous Mile 21s

■ The Boston Marathon is the world's oldest annual marathon, and arguably the most famous and prestigious. One of the Abbott World Marathon Majors, and the only one that necessitates a qualifying time, the race has inspired a whole culture of people competing just to run this race! At Mile 21 sits Heartbreak Hill, the most notorious of marathon obstacles. Since it comes so late in the race, runners must strategize how to overcome the dreaded uphill on a pair of severely fatigued legs.

■ No building is more recognizable in all of Russia than Saint Basil's Cathedral in Moscow's Red Square. Located across the block from the Kremlin, the church and museum, built in 1555 at the bequest of Ivan the Terrible, presides over Mile 21 of the Moscow Marathon. Pro tip: Bring your medal back for a postrace photo op to really beef up your Instagram game.

■ While hills, dirt roads, and winding paths are common in marathons, very few include large quantities of stairs. Enter the Great Wall Marathon, held yearly outside of Beijing, and run on a section of the Great Wall of China that includes plenty of centuries-old stone stairs. The challenging course returns to a portion of the wall for a final time in Mile 21, often pushing wiped-out runners onto their hands and knees as they struggle up and down China's greatest landmark.

✔ BODY CHECK — Chafing

Marathons boast a smorgasbord of gross bodily disturbances, but none is so uniquely and disgustingly "marathoning" than men with bloody nipples. After more than three hours of rubbing against cloth, the male nipple is raw and dribbling out blood. Not a good look, gents. How to fix it? Marathon coach Greg McMillan says, "Get dressed from the skin out." Make sure whatever is touching your skin for 26.2 miles is something your skin wants to be there. Tape those nipples, and be aware of the parts of your body that you know will chafe. Women especially experience friction between their thighs, so lube up with Vaseline or anti-chafe guards.

When picking out clothes for race day, only wear things you've trained in. Don't break out your race shirt just to realize a tag is scraping up your back. Be detail-oriented in your contingencies as well. What will you wear if it rains? Snows? Is 75 degrees? Pick out (and train in) all your options so you aren't pulling your sister's old windbreaker out of the closet at 6:00 a.m., praying it doesn't give you a rash. ■

roundup:
WORST MILE OF THE MARATHON

- Mile 1. You've just got to get through it.
  – *Shalane Flanagan*
- Mile 1. You're just getting your legs going.
  – *Dr. Mark Cucuzzella*
- Mile 1. You've still got 25 to go. – *Amby Burfoot*
- Mile 10. You still have more than 10 miles to go.
  – *Kat Wang*
- Mile 14. You've done half, and you have to do it all over. – *Lindsay Crouse*
- Mile 16. – *Greg McMillan*
- Mile 16. That's the one where you really learn what the race is going to hold. – *Kate Carter*
- Mile 17. You've gone so far, but you have so far to go. – *Bridget Quinn*
- Mile 18. If you're having a bad race, this mile is where it hits you. – *Amanda McGrory*
- Mile 19. You've gone so far, but you have the worst miles ahead. – *Danielle Quatrochi*
- Mile 20. – *Curt Munson*
- Mile 21. Most people only run 20 miles in training, so it's uncharted territory.
  – *Brinda Ayer*
- Mile 21. You feel like death, but still have five miles to go. – *Matthew Huff*
- Mile 22. That's when it starts to get really hard.
  – *Des Linden*
- Mile 23. I'm suffering really badly at that point.
  – *Michal Kapral*
- Mile 24. – *Meb Keflezighi*
- Mile 25. – *Dave Obelkevich*
- No such thing. Every mile is a great teacher with wonderful lessons. – *Apolo Ohno*

Running along with London Marathon Panda *Kate Carter*

You see a lot of things watching a marathon. A panda is not usually one of them, but at the 2019 London Marathon, Kate Carter ran the full 26.2 miles dressed in a panda costume. She finished in 3:48:32, earning the Guinness World Record for fastest marathon in a full-body animal costume (female). Kate, who has been obsessed with pandas since childhood, got the idea from her friend Sarah, who had earned the Guinness World Record for fastest woman in a wedding dress a few years prior. And, as Kate puts it, "If I was going to run as a panda, it could only be to raise money to help out the real ones," so she ran for the World Wildlife Fund, raising more than $1,200 for the charity. Here are her answers to my burning panda-related questions.

What is the process like for earning a Guinness World Record?

Guinness has a special partnership with the London Marathon, so you just sign up online and submit your application—you have to say what category you want to go for and send photos of yourself in costume. There are quite strict rules—for instance, the first panda head I found didn't quite cover my full face, so it was rejected. On the day itself, all the costume runners have to sign in at a special tent before the start to check the costumes again (in case you've sneakily tried to change it!). Along the course there are lots of "spotters" checking that runners are staying in their costumes for the full 26.2 miles.

Where did you get the panda costume, and how did you determine it was the best one to run 26.2 miles in?

Everyone asks me if it was specially made or technical material. Actually, I bought it on Amazon! It's a completely standard costume. You have to submit the costume quite far in advance, so I hadn't actually run a step in it at that point. I was quite definitely winging it!

Did you do any training specifically with the costume?

I did absolutely no running in it until I got back from the Boston Marathon, about a week before London. I then did a park run in it—so 5K—and the body was fine, if hot, but the head was a nightmare. It moved around so much that I couldn't see a thing. The night before the race I was up far too late trying different things and jogging around my kitchen to see if they worked. I ended up wearing a cap underneath the head, then pinning them together, and then wearing a hairband to hold the cap in place. I actually ran the entire marathon with a roll of duct tape around my wrist (sorry, paw) in case I had to do emergency taping! I still have no idea how it worked, but marathon magic happened.

What was the most difficult part about running the marathon in a costume?

Absolutely the overheating and limited vision. I was aware of being hot after a mile or two, but at Mile 18 or 19, I started to feel really weird, which in retrospect was overheating. Luckily, the head allowed me to drink without stopping and the London Marathon had little bottles with a spout, so they were easier to drink from.

What was the best or most rewarding part of running as a panda?

Honestly, it was one of the most amazing experiences of my life. I can't explain how incredible the crowd support was. Every single person seemed to cheer for me. I felt like I had all the benefits of being a massive celebrity—everyone loving you!—without any of the drawbacks. I was completely anonymous inside the costume. Also, I've become a minor celebrity at my children's school playground. Being in the Guinness World Records book has considerable clout in the preteen demographic.

If someone were to beat your world record, would you attempt to take it back?

Definitely!

MILE 22

Supporters

If you've never run a marathon before, it's hard to explain the overwhelming emotions you will feel, especially in the last few miles when your brain is semifried. You are hurting. You are tired. You are fighting with everything you've got just to cross that finish line, and, most of the time, you are completely alone. It's just you and your thoughts.

That is what makes having supporters so special, especially in miles like this one. When you're at your lowest of lows, to come around the corner and see your friends and family screaming your name is powerful. They've dragged themselves out in the cold at the crack of dawn and traipsed all around this city for you. They've gone to Walmart and bought giant poster boards and stayed up late the night before making signs to encourage you. They've been refreshing that tracking app and scanning the crowd for the last 40 minutes looking for your face.

When they see you, they go ballistic with whistles and shrieks and cowbells, and you can't help but dig deep down for every last ounce of energy to keep going because these people love and care about and believe in you! That is a powerful thing, especially when you're in a dark place, and it hits you right in the feels. There's no better feeling, folks, and that's why you're out here, and that's why you're going to finish this race.

<< New York City Marathon, New York, USA, 2013

Famous Mile 22s

- Marathon course designers love sending runners near tall structures, and there's nothing taller than Dubai's Burj Khalifa. The 2,722-foot-tall skyscraper looms over Mile 22 of the Dubai Marathon, a shiny needle in the sky. Luckily, marathon entrants just run past the base and not down the side of the building like Tom Cruise did in *Mission: Impossible–Ghost Protocol*.

- The largest marathon on Canada's West Coast, the Vancouver Marathon treats runners to a point-to-point tour of the city's downtown and picturesque bayside parks. As the marathon grinds along toward the finish, it passes through the city's famous Stanley Park. Mile 22 follows the coast as the race rounds the peninsular park as it juts into Burrard Inlet.

- African safari-goers often come in search of "the big five," or the lion, leopard, rhinoceros, elephant, and Cape buffalo. South Africa's Big Five Marathon takes its name from the formidable quintet and leads runners through a real African game reserve. It advertises "no fences" on its website as ideal for getting an up-close view of a baby elephant, but it's also terrifying when you think about racing a hungry lion on Mile 22 legs.

✔ BODY CHECK — Black Toenails

You aren't a true marathoner until you've had at least one toenail turn black and fall off. (Shocking more people don't run marathons, right?) The black toenail, or subungual hematoma for nerds, is caused by blood collecting underneath the toenail as a result of repeated trauma to the toe. Marathon coach Greg McMillan says not trimming your toenails or wearing shoes that are too tight in the toebox are two of the most common factors, but after 20-plus miles, sometimes toenails just turn black despite our best efforts. The good news is that usually they don't hurt much and heal themselves in time. The bad news is you could have gnarly-looking feet for a while. If something more serious (walking pain, an infection, etc.) occurs, you should see a doctor. I read one blog post that suggested a home remedy of stabbing a flaming hot paper clip through the top of your toenail to puncture undernail blisters (like melting your toenail!), but that sounds *horrific* so please don't do that. ▪

PR: the acronym for *personal record*, meaning your own fastest marathon time

Since the vast majority of us are not running marathons for that sweet prize money (apologies if I'm underestimating your prowess), our only real competition is our previous selves. Most marathoners know their PR down to the second and, aside from maybe a BQ, are simply trying to get a new PR with each marathon they run. Note that PR is now used as a verb as well as a noun, as in not only "I am going for a PR," but also "I'm going to PR." The great part about running your first marathon is that you automatically PR!

"I saw the clock coming down the homestretch and knew I was going to PR!"

Virtual Marathons

In 2018, the New York City Marathon announced that anyone who wanted to could run the race. No lottery. No qualification. No time cutoffs. The catch? You wouldn't actually be running on the racecourse. You'd be running wherever you wanted (Wisconsin, Poland, the moon—all fine) and using an app to track your progress. Thus, the first ever Virtual New York City Marathon was born.

Now, if you're asking yourself who would want to run 26.2 miles without the fans, the aid stations, and the inspirational finish in Central Park, you are not alone. For most, a virtual marathon is not an ideal experience, but more and more races have been adding them to their lineups. Runners still earn a T-shirt and medal, they still get the accomplishment of finishing a race, and they don't have to travel, qualify, or pay the same high entrance fee that someone running the physical race would.

While these races are much more popular in the 5K and half-marathon distances, virtual marathons became especially popular in the spring of 2020 during the coronavirus pandemic. With so many races being canceled, those who had been training took to the streets of their own neighborhoods to crank out 26.2 while social distancing. Nothing can compare to the power of pounding the pavement with thousands of other runners, but when life happens, it's good to know the marathon is always there if you're brave enough to run it.

Marathon Proposals: Dos and Don'ts

Looking to pop the question to the love of your life and attending a marathon in the near future? There may be some temptation to combine the two big days and propose on race day. No, this is not for everyone, but you'd be surprised how many couples get betrothed during the 26.2. Here are some dos and don'ts, just in case you're ready for marriage.

☐ **Do propose if you're the runner.** If this is your event and you don't care about potentially screwing up your time or taking attention away from your achievement, then go for it! Pop the question.

☐ **Don't propose if you're the bystander.** The person you're proposing to spent months training for this race. Don't lessen their accomplishment by slowing them down or stealing their thunder.

☐ **Do propose if your significant other doesn't care about looks (*and you know this for a fact*).** No one looks good after sweating for four hours.

☐ **Don't propose if you have any inkling that they might want hot proposal pics.** Pictures last forever!

☐ **Do propose to your significant other at the finish line.** Getting engaged during an important life moment is classic, and everyone's already so happy, so why not?

☐ **Don't propose to your significant other during the middle of the race.** This is a timed event, so it will slow the runner down. Also, the runner won't be able to focus on the remainder of the race.

☐ **Do propose if you're both seasoned runners.** The 10th marathon could use some spicing up.

☐ **Don't propose if this is your first marathon.** Spread the memories out.

☐ **Definitely don't propose anywhere between Mile 20 and the finish.** Just let the poor runner finish their race!

☐ **Definitely definitely don't propose if either of you has had to use a port-o-john during the race.** It's just no longer romantic.

Fun Marathon Signs

There's no better excuse to get crafty than as a marathon spectator. Racecourses are usually lined with adoring friends and family members waving homemade signs, so break out the posterboard, glitter, and magic markers. Here are a few of my favorites.

THEY TOWED MY CAR FOR THIS?	Pain is temporary; Instagram pics are forever.	Go, Mom, go!	That's a lot of work for a banana.
F**k yeah!	This pain isn't as bad as a kidney stone.	[giant fathead of the runner]	You're inspiring!
HURRY UP, I WANT TO GET TO BRUNCH.	WHAT A BUNCH OF SHOW-OFFS…	You Paid to Do This?	TOUCH HERE FOR POWER
CHUCK NORRIS NEVER RAN A MARATHON!	MORE COWBELL!	WE LOVE YOU, PERFECT STRANGER.	Always give 100%! (Unless you're giving blood)
HURRY UP, WE WANT TO GO TO THE BEACH.	GREAT JOB! Not you, I don't even know you!	Hurry up so we can DRINK!	If Vanessa Carlton can go 1,000 miles, you can go 26.2.

MILE 23

Medical Issues

The final hour of the marathon is the most grueling due to standard wear and tear on the body. That is only heightened when there is an injury or medical issue at play. Got a bad knee? You can probably get through a 5K without too much trouble. Not so for the marathon, an event that will sniff out the slightest weakness in the body and magnify it. By Mile 23, that achy hip or bad back is going to be in full bloom.

In 2006, Meb Keflezighi ran the New York City Marathon with food poisoning. In 2007, he dropped out of the London Marathon because of a "big wound on the bottom of [his] foot." He ran the 2008 Olympic Trials with a stress fracture in his hip. Shalane Flanagan got dehydrated during the Los Angeles Olympic Trials and barely finished. She also got hypothermia in Boston in 2018. "I'd say hypothermia is the most excruciating pain I've ever felt," she says.

The most miserable part of the marathon, though, is that there is no easy fix for these kinds of issues. You've got two choices: either keep going knowing that the pain will get worse or quit. It really comes down to mental toughness, determination, and grit. In the end, there's just your body and your mind, and these final miles are all about what your mind can trick your body into enduring.

<< Shenzhen International Marathon, China, 2014

193

Famous Mile 23s

■ Completed in 1933, the India Gate in New Delhi stands as a war memorial to the British Indian forces that died in World War I. Now it also serves as an axis point of the New Delhi Marathon. The 13-mile course, which is run twice, places the red stone arch at its center, with runners passing it four times—the final time during Mile 23—on their push to the finish line.

■ During the Stockholm Marathon, racers pass Stockholm City Hall multiple times, one of which is from all the way across the Riddarfjärden. At Mile 23, headed toward the finish inside the city's Olympic Stadium, runners trace the outside of the imposing architectural masterpiece for the final time. The City Hall, no stranger to grand events, also hosts the yearly Nobel Prize banquet.

■ One of only a few marathons run completely inside a national park, the Death Valley Marathon exiles runners into the Californian desert for 26.2 miles. The race, run in one of the hottest, driest sections of the United States, is so dangerous that only 350 marathoners are allowed to participate each year. While there are aid stations, runners are encouraged to wear water packs so they don't get dehydrated. Oh, and the road you're running on isn't closed to motor vehicles. This race is not for the faint of heart.

MARATHON VOCAB WORD

DNF: the acronym for *did not finish*, applied to runners who start a marathon but don't cross the finish line

Truly one of the most heartbreaking acronyms in running culture, DNF means that something didn't go your way. Unlike a DNS (did not start), which could imply all kinds of great things that kept you from the marathon (perhaps you won a free trip to Antigua!), a DNF means you crossed the start line with every intention of finishing and yet you couldn't. Most DNFs are the result of some physical ailment or another—a knee injury, back injury, ankle injury, dehydration, hypothermia, or just plain old fatigue. Sometimes they are the result of poor training, but often the injuries are unforeseeable. While it sucks to drop out of the race, sustaining a long-term injury is much worse, so feel no shame if this particular race day isn't yours. Even pros regularly get DNFs. Go home, get some rest, and start training again. There is always next year.

"I had to drop out after I spilled Gatorade in my eye, so I showed up as a DNF for that race."

✔️ BODY CHECK — Hyponatremia

Never heard of hyponatremia? Not surprising. According to Dr. George Chiampas, the marathon is "typically the only environment in which you see that condition. It's not something you typically see in a hospital setting or day to day." So what is it? He describes it as "dropping the salt content in your blood to a dangerous level." Sodium helps regulate the amount of water in your body, so if you don't have enough salt, your body retains more water and you run into problems (the worst of which is rapid brain swelling—yikes!). Basically, in the final miles of the marathon, if you're drinking too much water, on the course for a prolonged period of time, and are a salty sweater, you can lose too much sodium in your body. To prevent this problem, make sure you're taking in more than just water, especially if you're finishing in the five-plus-hour range or if it's a hot day. ▪

> *"In the end, there's just your body and your mind, and these final miles are all about what your mind can trick your body into enduring."*

Why People Quit

The worst part of any marathon is that there are people who can't finish it. Getting through that final .2 and crossing the finish is empowering and jubilant, but every marathon results sheet comes with rows of DNFs at the bottom of the list. So why don't people finish? Here are some reasons someone might end up as a DNF.

☐ **Didn't show up:** Signing up for a marathon is easy. Training for one is not. I cannot tell you how many people I know who have signed up for one, got a few days into training, and then decided the sport was not for them.

☐ **Didn't train properly:** The biggest factor for dropping out is not training properly. If your body isn't prepared for this grueling battle, then it is not going to be fun.

☐ **Couldn't make the time cutoff:** Many marathons have time cutoffs because of road closures. If you're a slow runner, be aware of these; if you don't go fast enough, you'll be picked up in the sweep bus and sent home.

☐ **Got injured:** Marathons are long races with a lot of variables. People get stepped on, trip, or run into things. It's easy to get injured if you're not focused.

☐ **Inappropriate behavior:** Races have rules, and race officials can yank you off the course if you're flashing people or shouting obscenities, but they can also cut you if your costume doesn't fit race standards, if your bib isn't on, or if you're carrying prohibited items.

☐ **Aggravated an old injury:** Training for a marathon puts a lot of stress on the body, and sometimes the taper before the race can make you think everything is healed. Old injuries and chronic health problems have a habit of rearing their ugly heads, though, so take it easy even if you feel good at the start.

☐ **Dehydration:** A perennial favorite. If you're not drinking water on a cool day, it can get you; on a hot day, dehydration runs rampant.

☐ **Not feeling it:** Plenty of people quit because it's painful to run 26.2 miles. They aren't injured or dehydrated. They just decide it's too much trouble, and their desire to not be running is stronger than their desire to finish.

☐ **Death:** While it's rare, there are people who die while running marathons every year. Unknown heart defects and cardiac arrests are among the most common causes. While marathons have top-notch medical staff on-site to deal with these calamities, sometimes there is nothing they can do. This is why you should always consult a doctor before starting a new exercise routine, especially if it's marathon running.

☐ **Life event:** Life goes on even during a marathon, and there are people who have found out midrace about an emergency and had to quit. There will always be another marathon, and some things are more important.

☐ **A baby:** To end on a happier note, your wife could go into labor while you're running the race. Surprise! You'd better redirect that course to the hospital. You're going to be a parent!

Marathons at the Olympics

There is perhaps no sport more closely tied to the Olympic Games than the marathon. The first ever marathon race (not including the ancient Greek war story) was invented for the original Olympics back in 1896. Even the bizarre race length was created because of the Olympics. (More on that on page 227.) There has never been a modern Olympics without the marathon, and the marathon would not exist without the Olympics. Here are some fun facts and tidbits concerning this intertwined duo.

The Last Day
It is Olympic tradition that the men's marathon is run on the morning of the final day of competition, an iconic calendar placement. It is made only more impressive by the fact that the medals are often given out during the closing ceremony, a global showcase event attended by heads of state, celebrities, and all other Olympic athletes, rather than in a traditional medal ceremony like every other sport.

Olympic Stadium
While not always the case, most Olympic marathons end inside the Olympic Stadium, creating a historic conclusion as runners make a final lap around the track to finish their race. With many stadiums being repurposed after the games, these are one-of-a-kind finishes. During the 2012 games in London, however, organizers elected to finish near Buckingham Palace in the same place the traditional London Marathon ends.

Olympic Record
With vastly different courses, altitude, and weather at each games, comparing marathon times across Olympics can be a futile effort. Consider the difference between running in Atlanta, Georgia, and Helsinki, Finland, during the heat of summer. That being said, here are the speediest winners to finish the 26.2.

- **MEN: Samuel Wanjiru** (Kenya), 2:06:32, *Beijing Olympics, 2008*
- **WOMEN: Tiki Gelana** (Ethiopia), 2:23:07, *London Olympics, 2012*

Medal Count

Total Medals *(Male and Female):*	Total Gold Medals *(Male and Female):*
1. United States: 13	1. Ethiopia: 6
2. Kenya: 12	2. United States: 4
3. Ethiopia: 11	3. France: 3
4. Japan: 9	4. Kenya: 3

Female Olympians
While the men's marathon has been around since the games' inception, the women's marathon was only added in 1984 for the Los Angeles Olympics. Traditionally held during the middle Sunday of the games, the women's marathon is run separately from the men's, a distinction rarely seen in other races.

Running along with Marathon Medical Director *George Chiampas*

If you're healthy and cruise through the 26.2 without incident, you may never notice the marathon's medical team. In fact, the numerous doctors, nurses, and volunteers monitoring the race hope you never need to visit them. When tragedy strikes, however, there is no more important group on the course.

Dr. George Chiampas has served as the medical director of the Chicago Marathon since 2007. With a background in sports medicine and emergency medicine, he's a natural fit for the role. Working year-round, he and his team are responsible for the safety of nearly 50,000 marathoners who run the race each year. They think through (and plan meticulously for) the worst-case scenarios so runners don't have to. The behind-the-scenes work is awe-inspiring!

What does the medical team for the Chicago Marathon look like?

We have more than 2,000 medical volunteers. That's 150 to 200 physicians, 250 to 300 nurses, physical therapists, massage therapists, athletic trainers, psychologists, social workers, and EMTs. Under all of those categories, we also have students in each discipline. We work with a private ambulance company that provides nearly 50 ambulances across the course and finish area in a coordinated fashion. We have 12 golf carts, 10 bike teams, and additional teams on foot. All of this is supplemented by the Chicago Fire Department. The medical program is core in our vision.

Where on the course are all these volunteers?

We have 21 medical tents on the course. They range from teams of 8 to 12 people near the beginning to 16 to 20 people later on. We also have mobile teams of 200 to 300 people monitoring the area before and after the finish. There are two large main medical tents, which can house 120 patients in one and 80 in the other. There are around 200 to 300 medical staff members per tent.

How do you organize such a massive staff?

We operate a unified command approach that we call the Chicago model. We bring all the stakeholders—from the city, state, public health, Chicago Police, Chicago Fire, federal authority, state authority, etc.—into a command center. Every decision maker is within the command center to not only operate the event, but also allow the city to function in the same manner on race day. Our event has led globally, and other races have replicated our model.

What are the most common reasons a runner would visit the medical team?

The most common is a muscular or bone issue. That can range from someone who has a muscle strain or some soreness that gets aggravated to someone who could potentially break their hip while running or someone who has a stress fracture and that day ends up being the breaking point.

Outside of marathon day itself, what does the role of medical director entail?

When the race finishes, we have wrap-up meetings and inventory our supplies to determine what we need for the following year. We build our inventory and brainstorm innovative ideas we'd like to try out in the future. We collect a lot of data each year—we see where the runners are coming in along the course and what types of injuries they have—and we build a plan based off that for the next year. We recruit and train our volunteers. We collaborate a lot with other marathons. We travel to other events, share best practices, give talks, and partner with our local state and city agencies on different events that occur here. We also collaborate with our police department, fire department, and office of emergency management.

How does race day start for you?

My day starts with hyping up our medical volunteers, really making sure they feel invigorated and connected to the runners. I remind them every year that, for runners, the medical team is sort of an afterthought and you only appreciate them when you need them. But I remind our medical staff that we have thousands and thousands of runners that are running and raising millions of dollars for various charities, and most of the time those charities have something to do with a medical cause. Many of our volunteers are the runners' physicians, physical therapists, or clinicians, and I remind them that they've walked the runners to that start line and been a part of that journey. We're all pulling in the same direction, and when the runners cross that finish line, hopefully we're crossing with them.

MILE 24 Not Caring

You start a marathon with plenty of goals and standards: I want to finish in under four hours. I want to make a new PR. I want to run without walking. I don't want to throw up on a bystander.

By Mile 24, all those wonderful goals and promises are out the window. At this point, the only thing that matters is finishing, and by hook or by crook, you're going to drag yourself across that finish line. Who cares what you look like? Who cares what your time is? Who cares if you've got blood streaming down the front of your shirt because you didn't tape those nipples? (I told you so.) Just get to the end of this godforsaken race.

Some races you'll feel better than others, but if you've had a bad race, especially if it's hot, you won't have the energy to care about anything other than ending this agony. During a particularly hot Marine Corps Marathon, I both threw up on my shoes and peed (right out there in the open) in the Pentagon parking lot. Am I proud of those facts now? No. But at the time, I was too tired to care or look for a port-o-john. That is where the marathon takes you, and yet somehow we keep signing up for more.

<< Rotterdam Marathon, The Netherlands, 2013

☑ BODY CHECK — Public Health

In 2020, most marathons were canceled under the threat of the coronavirus. The Monterey Bay Half-Marathon was canceled in 2018 due to poor air quality during the California wildfires. The 2012 New York City Marathon was canceled after Hurricane Sandy damaged the infrastructure needed for a safe race. Beyond the individual race-related medical issues that marathon organizers are aware of, public health is also a huge part of the marathon. Dr. George Chiampas says that public health concerns like the Zika virus or influenza definitely impact their events: "We have to be cognizant of what's going on globally because we are a global event on a global stage." Especially in the weakened state of a marathoner's body postrace, diseases can be lethal. While outbreaks like the coronavirus are rare, the flu is not, so make sure you're prepped for common health concerns, which can be heightened by the 26.2. ■

Famous Mile 24s

■ If you like running toward mountains rather than up them, check out the Jackson Hole Marathon, held annually in the Wyoming Valley near Yellowstone. The Mile 24 view includes Grand Teton towering over the horizon—but don't worry, the race ends before you get there.

■ Amsterdam is known for its canals, and fittingly, runners in the Amsterdam Marathon will spend plenty of time running alongside them. Mile 24 concludes a long stretch of the course following Singelgracht—the canal, whose name means "to surround"—which encircles the city's center. Also along that mile is the Rijksmuseum, a massive art museum housing Dutch masterpieces from the Golden Age.

■ Unlike Antarctica, which is a continent made of land, the North Pole is nothing but a giant chunk of frozen ice floating in the Arctic Ocean. Setting up the course for the North Pole Marathon can be difficult, as breaks in the ice and safety concerns have to be managed. At Mile 24, the runners should be nearing their final loop of what is usually a short course run 10 or more times. However many loops, though, you'll still finish at the North Pole. Tell Santa I said hi!

runchies: food cravings resulting from running long distances

This word is another portmanteau, this time of *run* and *munchies*. When you run a lot, you get really hungry. A marathon burns off more than 2,500 calories, so after the race you're going to need to eat, and after avoiding junk food and alcohol during parts of your training, you deserve whatever you've been craving. Here are some suggestions: Olive Garden's Tour of Italy, a dozen Krispy Kreme doughnuts, a Jimmy John's sub, a Culver's ButterBurger with cheese curds and a root beer, Little Caesars Crazy Bread, the family-size bag of Gardetto's, anything dipped in ranch dressing, several king-sized KitKat bars, chicken fingers from Sticky's, or a Starbucks S'mores Frappuccino.

"I had such bad runchies after the race that I ate four bananas before I even got out of the finish area."

BQ's MARATHON HISTORY
Boston Strong

On the afternoon of April 15, 2013, at the 117th running of the Boston Marathon, two homemade bombs exploded near the finish line, killing three people and maiming hundreds. Seventeen of those injured lost limbs. Spectators Jessica Kensky, an oncology nurse, and Patrick Downes, a doctoral student in clinical psychology specializing in children, were two of those who lost legs. Both were marathoners. They were also newlyweds. Both lost their left legs in the blast, and later Kensky would have her severely injured right leg amputated as well. The challenges—physical, emotional, and practical—were immense, but the couple has kept on marathoning. One year after the bombing, Kensky won the Boston 2014 women's handcycle race in 2:14:13, crossing the finish hand in hand with her husband, who finished 17th in the men's division. Downes competed on a handcycle again the following year, and in 2016 he became the first Boston bombing amputee to run across the finish line of the Boston Marathon on a prosthetic running blade.

Marathon Security

In the early days, marathon security was nonexistent. Sure, maybe the race organizers would throw a doctor or two out on the course, but aside from that, there was little reason to be concerned and even fewer resources to spare. Heck, some early marathons didn't even have aid stations or completely closed streets. Even as recently as the 2004 Olympics, security was lax enough for a defrocked Irish priest in a kilt to tackle the leader Vanderlei de Lima into the crowd midrace.

But the bombing of the Boston Marathon in 2013—where two homemade pressure cooker bombs were detonated near the race's finish—completely shifted the way race organizers viewed marathon security. Much like airports were completely overhauled after 9/11, massive changes were instituted following Boston.

Some of the most noticeable changes came in the form of restricted areas. Before 2013, most races (like old-school airports) allowed spectators and runners to roam willy-nilly. Anyone could watch the start and the finish. Big races would put up some barriers in places for crowd control, but otherwise it was the Wild West.

Since the bombs were planted near the Boston Marathon's finish line (a densely populated area of any race), marathon starts and finishes are now largely blocked off. In major marathons like Chicago, runners go through security to enter the starting area. The only bag they're allowed to bring is the clear one provided by the race. Gone are the days of sauntering over to the finish line as well. Watching the finish line has become a ticketed event at many marathons, and the postrace queues are heavily restricted to runners only. It can be another mile's walk before a marathoner reaches the public.

Aside from beefing up police presence at races and restricting spectator areas, marathons also have implemented rules about what runners can wear (no masks or bags), what spectators can bring (no large backpacks or duffels), and what types of watching activities are permitted (no rooftop parties). While these new rules may seem invasive, they work to keep the thousands of people who run marathons each year safe. With the sport continuing to grow, making sure every runner has a safe race from start to finish is vital.

MARATHONER

"By Mile 24 . . . the only thing that matters is finishing, and by hook or by crook, you're going to drag yourself across that finish line."

Running along with New York City Marathon Race Director *Jim Heim*

In 2019, 53,627 people finished the New York City Marathon, making it the world's largest marathon ever. The race, which featured runners from 141 countries and all 50 states, was viewed by more than one million spectators along the course. In addition, 125,000 people visited the race expo in the days before the race; 12,000 volunteers worked the event; and 150 entertainment acts lined the course. There were 37 medical aid stations, 57 ambulances, and 40 portable toilet locations along the course, which winds through all five of the city's boroughs. The New York City Marathon is one of the largest and most complicated events thrown each year, and helming the entire process is Jim Heim, the marathon's race director, who has worked with New York Road Runners since 2007. I spoke with him about everything that goes on behind the scenes.

This marathon is massive. What are some of the keys to planning such a huge event?

Everything we do is about relationships because we don't own a stadium. Turning New York City into a course for a day, and then turning it back into a city is an immense operation. It's not just us. The buy-in from the city and community makes the magic of this thing. The top three agencies we work with are the mayor's office, the New York Police Department, and the parks department.

What does race day look like for you and your team?

People look at the marathon as one event, but we look at it as several events. The start, finish, course, transportation, and expo are all separate megaevents unto themselves, so most of our team members only really see one. Even the start is two different events. There's Fort Wadsworth, the prestaging area, and we are building that for two to three weeks before the event. Then there's the bridge, the actual start line, and nothing happens there until midnight on race day. Everything we're going to build is all on a convoy that goes up on that bridge at midnight, and we basically have a six- to seven-hour window to build everything we need to build—the sound, audio, port-o-johns, stages, and TV setup. It all happens in a very small window.

What are some of the biggest changes that you've seen made to the race?

It's the largest marathon in the world, but it's also one of the most logistically complex. When I started back in 2007, we had around 37,000 people and we're up to 53,000 now. We didn't just do what we were doing before and add more people to it. We wanted to be sure the experience would be good. The introduction of wave starts was important. Another huge one was the Staten Island Ferry. Back in the day, everyone used to come over the Verrazzano-Narrows Bridge and be dropped off at the toll plaza. Now half the people come over on the ferry. We've been able to take the pressure way down on the bridge, which allowed us to grow.

Weather is obviously a big concern for all marathons. How do you plan for that?

It's rarely Plan A, so you have to have Plans B through G all ready to go. In 2014, we had significant wind, so the wheelchairs started in Brooklyn. The winds were too high for the Metropolitan Transportation Authority to be comfortable with sending them over the bridge. We also employ a meteorologist who is with us from two weeks out, and we talk every morning about what we're seeing and how we want to make adjustments.

What is the most surprising thing going on behind the scenes of the race?

Just the scope of the operation. The numbers are what stagger people. Nothing is out there on the course until 3:00 a.m., and an hour or so after the runners are gone, you'd have no idea anything was there. Our experience is larger than life.

MILE 25

The Walking Dead

By this point, any real threat of quitting (barring a terrible injury) has left your mind. You're going to finish. It's just a matter of gritting your teeth and getting there. It's only two miles, but it feels like 50.

And here's something they don't tell you. No one is cheering for you in Mile 25. Everyone wants to be at the finish, and logistically you can't watch your runner at both Mile 25 and 26, so the crowd is scant.

The joy of the race has evaporated, and what's left is a bunch of miserable people shuffling along in silence. All you can hear are trudging, lead-footed steps and panting. A pack of zombies smelling of body odor and Gatorade.

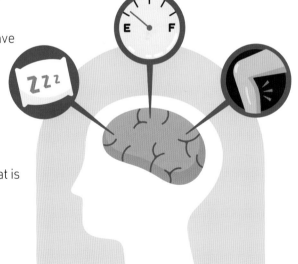

This is where Meb Keflezighi prays: "In the wilderness, I have the dialogue to say, 'God, I believe in you. Give me the strength to overcome whatever challenge I'm facing.' When I'm running, I think about my Christianity quite a bit."

For some reason, in these last few miles, music no longer motivates me. Frivolities don't matter. There is just you and the finish and whatever deep-rooted longing or purpose or need that is going to get you there. Keep praying and press on.

<< Marathon des Sables, Morocco, 2011 (see page 219)   Pages 208–209: Marine Corps Marathon, Washington, DC, USA, 2009

Famous Mile 25s

- As the Venice Marathon reaches its final miles, runners cross the Ponte della Libertà to enter the ancient city built on top of 118 small islands. At Mile 25 sits the Piazza San Marco, Venice's most recognizable public square, along with the iconic bell tower Campanile di San Marco. It should be noted, however, that at high tide the piazza often floods, so depending on the weather, you may be rerouted.

- After 25 miles crisscrossing Mexico's capital, the Mexico City Marathon finally makes its way to the Palacio de Bellas Artes. The theater and museum, which sit in the city's historic center across from Alameda Central, hosts opera, ballet, and theater as well as art exhibits. While runners won't be able to bask in the high arts inside, they will be treated to views of the hulking colonnades and fiery dome.

- Balboa Park in San Diego, California, has it all. Not only is it a beautiful 1,200-acre park with dozens of gardens, but it also houses the city's Air & Space, Art, and Natural History Museums. Perhaps its most famous landmark, though, is the San Diego Zoo, the most-visited zoo in the United States. Winding through these is Mile 25 of the San Diego Marathon, which bumps against the zoo and several museums as it nears the finish.

A Marathon in Under Two Hours

Since 1967, the world record for the men's marathon has been under 2:10:00, which has led countless people over the years to muse on if and when someone would finally run 26.2 in under two hours. As the record continued to drop over the years, people became more obsessed with breaking the barrier. In 2014, Kenyan Dennis Kimetto ran the Berlin Marathon in 2:02:57, and Nike decided it was going to lead the charge, launching Breaking2. Inviting three of the world's fastest runners to a closed (so not world-record-eligible) course, Nike set them up with elite pacers and new Nike Vaporfly Elite shoes. Eliud Kipchoge won the race with a time of 2:00:25, barely missing the cutoff. The shoes, however, stuck around and led Eliud to grab a new world record at Berlin in 2018 with a time of 2:01:39.

In May 2019, Eliud announced that he would be attempting to break two again, this time by himself in the carefully planned Ineos 1:59 Challenge. Pacing lasers guided the pacers, who ran in a "K" formation for drafting. The course was flat and lined with trees to prevent wind. It was at low altitude. Eliud wore a newer version of the Nike Vaporflys. Hydration was delivered to him on a bike. He finished in 1:59:40, which is not world-record eligible, but still pretty darn incredible. It's only a matter of time before someone does it in a race.

chip time: the time in between when your race chip crosses the starting line and the finish line (i.e., the time it took you to run the marathon)

Now that we've entered the computer age, race timing has become much more precise. Early marathons were run using "gun time," or the time between the starting gun's sounding and the time you, as the runner, crossed the finish line. If you weren't at the front of the pack, your finish time was inflated with however many minutes you spent milling around at the start. Now, however, a chip on your race bib registers your (or at least your bib's) exact time. While your chip time will show up on the official results website, all times posted on the course are gun times. If you want to accurately pace yourself on the course, and you aren't in Corral A, use your watch or phone to track your chip time.

"When I finished, the clock said four hours, so I knew I was close to 3:45 because my chip time would be faster."

 **BODY CHECK — Hallucinations**

If you see your long-dead grandmother cheering for you during Mile 25 of the marathon, fear not. It's not the zombie apocalypse. You're just hallucinating. While this is extremely rare in marathons (it's much more common in ultramarathons, which tend to enjoy sleep depriving their runners), it does occur for runners pushing toward 26.2, especially if you're pushing more than six hours on the course. The common causes (as with dizziness or fainting) are dehydration, lack of food, and heat. If you're at the point where you are seeing things, your vision is getting hazy, or you're experiencing tunnel vision, it's best to pop off at a medical tent for a bit. A break and some medical attention might slow down your time, but that's much better than passing out on the asphalt or accidentally hugging a stranger who you think is Granny Josephine. ■

Let's Make the Marathon a Sport

Except when referencing a village in Greece, the word *marathon* didn't exist in English until the late 19th century, when a modern Olympic movement influenced by romantic ideas in art revived the legend of the heroic Greek. (See "Pheidippides," where Robert Browning writes, "Joy in his blood bursting his heart, he / died—the bliss!" In a nice flourish, his Pheidippides dies not from exertion, but from joy.) With such inspiration, the first modern Olympics culminated in a 25-mile run from the Gulf of Marathon to Athens's Panathenaic Stadium, kicking off on April 10, 1896, at 2:00 p.m. Some 100,000 spectators lined the hot, dusty route to witness the contest—won by native son Spyridon Louis, who paused partway for wine or cognac (accounts vary). Yamas! When Louis entered the stadium, the princes of Greece leapt from the stands to escort their hero to the finish line in 2:58:50.

MILE 26 Picking It Back Up

Only a mile to go! You can do a mile. You've run hundreds, if not thousands, of them in your life. Hell, you could crawl a mile if you needed to. You could push your car a mile. You could push your car while crawling a mile! And this is where it clicks that you're almost there. You're going to finish. You've got mere minutes until this is all over and you're sucking down Gatorade with that big, beautiful, glistening medal hanging around your neck.

In Mile 25, you could have sworn your body parts were about to pop off and roll into the gutter, but now that pain is lessening. You've somehow got more energy. You're—dare we say it?—smiling.

Three-quarters of a mile left now. That's like seven minutes left. Less, if you can pick up the pace, and *you can pick it up*. Where was all this energy back in Mile 22, huh?

Half a mile to go. You could literally die right here and still roll to the finish. You can hear noise up ahead. Is that the crowd at the finish line? *Gah!* Let's go faster! Come on! We can pass a few of these people.

And there is that bloody miraculous "Mile 26" marker! The people are shouting! What a spectacular day to be alive!

<< *Berlin Marathon, Germany, 2011*   **Pages 214–215:** *New York City Marathon, New York, USA, 2011*

☑ BODY CHECK — The Final Push

In Mile 24, you feel like you've got nothing left to give. Will you finish? Unlikely. Will you die on the streets of Baltimore to be ground into the pavement and oblivion by the trotting feet of thousands? Almost certainly. Now, not 30 minutes later, you feel somehow lighter, stronger, exuberant. What gives? Turns out it's the pesky brain again. Marathon coach Greg McMillan sums it up: "The mind changes from 'Oh my gosh, I'm not sure I can' to 'Hey, I'm going to be able to do that.' You can see how mentally that is a totally different mindset. When your mind starts to go, 'I can do that,' it allows you to keep pushing." Greg cites Tim Noakes's Central Governor Theory, which claims that when your brain senses danger, it actively tries to make you uncomfortable to get you to decrease exertion. When the brain knows the finish line is only eight minutes away, it turns off those pain sensors, allowing you to power on through to the finish. ■

MARATHON VOCAB WORD

ultramarathoner:

someone who has run a distance longer than 26.2 miles

So, you're a marathoner. What's next? How about an ultramarathon? Technically speaking, any event longer than a marathon counts, so if you do a 27-miler, you're in ultra territory. The most common distances are 50K (31 miles), 100K (62 miles), and 100 miles, but some ultramarathons are run on time instead of distance (i.e., how far can you run in six hours? 12 hours? 24 hours?). While there are ultramarathon street races, they tend to exist most commonly in the trail-running community. It should be noted that the Ironman doesn't technically constitute an ultramarathon; since you only run 26.2 miles, it is really just a long triathlon. Fun fact: In 1988, a man named Yiannis Kouros ran 1,000 miles in 10 days and 10 hours. That's like running from New York to Minneapolis. Just thinking about it is giving me the runchies.

"I dropped my phone in the marathon and had to run a few yards backward to pick it up, so technically I'm an ultramarathoner."

What's Longer Than a Marathon?

Marathon not long enough, you say? Give me more, my legs are mighty! I need to push my body to the brink, and 26.2 miles is not cutting the mustard! Well, here are some longer, nastier, more grueling endurance events to put yourself through—a masochist's row of ultramarathons.

☐ **Dances with Dirt:** Run through hell. Hell, Michigan, that is. Traverse wooded hills for either 50K (31 miles) or 50 miles along forest trails. Trail runs are already harder than marathons due to the terrain, and tacking on another 5 or 24 miles will make this race a whole new experience.

☐ **Spartathlon:** Athens to Marathon not enough? What about Athens to Sparta? This ultra is a 153-mile race that includes 75 checkpoints to knock out runners who are too slow or too tired to continue. The course record is 20 hours, 25 minutes.

☐ **Badwater Ultramarathon:** At 135 miles, this race is technically shorter than the Spartathlon. However, it is run in the heat of July in Death Valley, where temperatures can reach 130 degrees Fahrenheit. Oh, and it has a cumulative elevation gain of more than 19,000 feet.

☐ **Barkley Marathons:** Only 15 runners have ever finished this bizarre race. With 60 hours to finish the 60-mile course, this ultra appears easy on paper, but the whole event—from its registration fee (a license plate) to its start (the race director's lighting of a cigarette any time between midnight and noon)—is bizarre. The course is run through the backwoods of Tennessee's Frozen Head State Park, is marked solely by books hidden in the forest, and changes each year.

☐ **Marathon des Sables:** Often called the toughest footrace on earth, this is a six-day trek across the Moroccan Sahara Desert. The course may be only 156 miles, but have you ever tried to run on sand in the African desert? Not a good time.

☐ **World Marathon Challenge:** Seven marathons in seven days on seven continents. Not only is that a lot of running, but it's also a lot of time on an airplane—not a great recovery environment.

☐ **Burro Days:** Every year in Fairplay, Colorado, there is a 29-mile ultramarathon. The catch is you're running along with a burro (i.e., a donkey). Without riding it, you have to coax the stubborn animal along the full course. If he doesn't move, neither do you.

Running along with Olympic Speedskater *Apolo Ohno*

Apolo Ohno has eight Olympic medals, not to mention a few dozen from world championships. He competed in three separate Olympics on the US short track speedskating team, and then went on to win *Dancing with the Stars*, become a sports commentator, and raise money for numerous charities. He most certainly has nothing to prove by running 26.2 miles, but he ran the New York City Marathon in 2011 anyway, crushing his debut in an impressive 3:25. Here are his thoughts about trying a whole new sport on for size.

After years as a professional speedskater, what initially made you want to run a marathon?

As a short track speedskater, anything over two minutes and 15 seconds of intensity always seemed alien to me. Upon retirement, I knew it was time to start new challenges and push my body into areas it was not familiar with (i.e., endurance training).

As someone used to intense athletic training, how did training for a marathon compare to training as a speedskater?

The training was significantly different. First, it was much less intense in terms of brute force output. However, the repetition and mileage was something that my body was just not used to, and it took time for the adaptation to sink in. The only similarity is what happens in your mind when you start to tire.

You finished the New York City Marathon in 3:25, which is an impressive time. What was your biggest challenge in the race?

The biggest challenge was that my calves started to cramp around Mile 20. The most rewarding part was actually the last six miles, both because I felt those were the most difficult and because the area of New York that you get to finish in—Central Park—is amazing and full of energy and fans.

What is it like running as a public figure? Did people recognize you during the race?

The journey was an interesting one, as I had been traveling every three days to new locations for events, business, and speaking engagements all over the country, so the training needed to be modified for such a wild travel schedule. On race day, people recognized me from the very start, and it was awesome! There were a lot of selfies and short chats to say hello.

Famous Mile 26s

■ The final of the six Abbott World Marathon Majors (along with New York, Boston, Chicago, Tokyo, and London, for review) is the Berlin Marathon, run every September in the German capital. In Mile 26, racers pass under the famed Brandenburg Gate, an 18th-century Prussian monument on the site of the former city gate. The gate was off-limits during the Cold War, but now it's open to all!

■ Just as pilgrims traveled miles to reach the abbey on Le Mont-Saint-Michel in France, so do the runners of the Mont Saint-Michel Marathon. The island commune off the coast of Normandy was built because of its highly defensible position. It is accessible on foot from the mainland at low tide, but safeguarded at high tide. Now marathoners nearing their goal run toward the island in their final mile.

■ Sure, you could sign up to run marathons in nine different countries around the world, but you could also just run the Walt Disney World Marathon, the final full mile of which winds through Epcot. Running through the park's World Showcase, you'll pass France, Morocco, Japan, Italy, Germany, China, Norway, and Mexico without ever opening your passport. Then run under Epcot's famed globe, and you're off to the finish line.

THE .2

The Finish

You turn the corner, and there it is: the finish line. There were times when you thought you'd never get there. There were times you considered quitting, when your body felt one step away from crumbling underneath you. Yet you made it. Now you can see the finish.

You're picking up speed, hurdling through these final steps, and the crowds are going ballistic on both sides of the course. They're screaming, ringing bells, waving posters, pounding on the barricades, and congratulating you on what you're about to accomplish—something most people never will.

As that finish banner gets closer, you're overwhelmed by what you've accomplished. When you decided to run 26.2, there were people who didn't think you could do it. Hell, you didn't think you could half the time, but you got up early before the sun rose, and you ran after long days at the office. You skipped nights drinking with your friends, survived blisters and lost toenails, and at this moment it all becomes worth it.

The crowds are cheering and your body is so tired, but you stream across that line with the biggest smile on your face because you did it! *You ran a marathon*!

<< Boston Marathon, Massachusetts, USA, 2017

223

> **"You skipped nights drinking with your friends, survived blisters and lost toenails, and at this moment it all becomes worth it."**

hardware: *what runners call their finisher medals and trophies*

Of the many reasons to run a marathon, the hardware is near the top. Race medals are insanely big and beautiful. They also change every year, so even if you've run a specific marathon once, returning gets you something new. Many marathons pride themselves on increasingly extravagant medals with moving pieces, secret compartments, and personal engraving. On par with having a fancy medal is wearing the fancy medal for the entire day of the race (and sometimes longer, but your mileage may vary on what's appropriate there). Wander to brunch with your medal around your neck and you're guaranteed to get kudos from your waiter. Live it up! You just ran a freaking marathon, so show off that bling!

"I'm installing a rack in our living room so I have a place to display all of my race hardware."

✔ BODY CHECK — Crying

While training for my first marathon, I envisioned crossing the finish line thousands of times. I'd be exuberant, with the world's largest grin, my arms outstretched, pride and elation oozing out of every atom of my body. Not once did I envision myself weeping as I ran down the final straightaway in downtown Detroit. And yet there are photos of me blubbering my way across the finish line.

And I'm not alone. For every smiling or exhausted finisher, there's one sobbing. Why? Because the marathon changes lives. Marathon coach Greg McMillan says, "The last hour of a marathon is a big, big challenge, which is why people are crying as they cross the finish. Mothers compare it to childbirth. It's this amazing, intense, 100 percent focus thing, and *you did it*! You crossed that finish line. You had that experience of really having to bring your A game."

Rarely in life, if ever, do people face something of this level of physical exertion that requires this amount of training. Just completing a marathon proves you can accomplish more than you previously thought you could. Finishing your first marathon is a once-in-a-lifetime experience, so you'll experience once-in-a-lifetime feelings (which include ugly crying). ■

roundup: FIRST MARATHON

- **New York City Marathon** – *Apolo Ohno, Shalane Flanagan, Greg McMillan, Meb Keflezighi, Bridget Quinn, Dave Obelkevich, and Brinda Ayer*
- **Boston Marathon** – *Des Linden, George Hirsch, Amby Burfoot, and Bennett Beach*
- **San Diego Rock 'n' Roll Marathon** – *Danielle Quatrochi and Kat Wang*
- **London Marathon** – *Ryan Hall and Kate Carter*
- **Detroit Marathon** – *Matthew Huff*
- **Marine Corps Marathon** – *Dr. Mark Cucuzzella*
- **Toronto Marathon** – *Michal Kapral*
- **Newport Marathon (Rhode Island)** – *Lindsay Crouse*

Famous Finishes

Marathon organizers love nothing more than an epic finish, so many have situated their finish lines near well-known landmarks. They're good for race photos, good for Instagram, and good for encouraging all the feels as you hustle through the final .2 miles. Here are some of the most epic marathon ending points.

■ The Niagara Falls Marathon, run in both New York and Canada, finishes alongside the Canadian Horseshoe Falls, which are definitely better than those on the US side.

■ The Bangkok Marathon in Thailand ends near Wat Phra Kaew (the Temple of the Emerald Buddha), the most sacred Buddhist temple in Thailand.

■ The marathon can be a bloody affair, so the Rome Marathon correctly positioned the Colosseum, an old gladiator arena, at its finish line.

- ■ The Seattle Marathon is here for your Instagram success. Snap a finisher pic with your medal and the city's famed Space Needle in the background as the race ends near its base.
- ■ While the London Marathon doesn't technically end at Buckingham Palace, it does circle past the front gates right before the end near St. James's Park.
- ■ The New York City Marathon spends its last few miles in Central Park before concluding near Tavern on the Green. The only way to be more iconically New York would be to end at the Statue of Liberty, but you have to take a boat to get there.
- ■ The world's most famous marathon, the Boston Marathon doesn't end near a famous landmark per se, but after 26 miles of trotting through the Massachusetts countryside, the city of Boston feels pretty incredible in and of itself.
- ■ When Pheidippides ran the first marathon from Marathon, he ended up in Athens, so finishing the Athens Marathon in the Panathenaic Stadium, in the city where the original endurance run ended, feels pretty special.
- ■ The Paris Marathon starts and ends at the Arc de Triomphe, which makes sense because running 26.2 miles really is a triumph in so many ways.
- ■ The Istanbul Marathon, which is the only marathon in the world to take place on two continents, finishes near the Hagia Sophia, the massive Byzantine cathedral turned mosque turned museum.
- ■ At the end of the Marine Corps Marathon in Washington, DC, is the Marine Corps War Memorial. Fashioned after the famous image of marines planting the flag after the Battle of Iwo Jima, the memorial serves as a fitting end to the race.
- ■ Running from downtown Los Angeles to the coast, Los Angeles Marathon runners finish near the Santa Monica boardwalk on the Pacific Ocean. Take a dip to cool off after the 26.2!

BQ's MARATHON HISTORY
Why the .2?

Until the London Olympics of 1908, there was no standard marathon distance. The race was understood to be "about 25 miles." In London, a 25-mile route was established from Windsor Castle to the Olympic Stadium, then adjusted to start on the castle's East Lawn, where royal children might oversee it from their nursery, and end before Queen Alexandra's Royal Box, requiring a half-lap of the stadium to finish. The race now measured 26 miles, 385 yards. For some reason, 26.2 stuck! What didn't stick was the apparent winner. Most spectators hoped anyone but an American would win, after the Americans refused to "dip" their flag to the royals at the opening ceremony, proclaiming, "This flag dips to no earthly king." So, when Italian Dorando Pietri entered the stadium first, cheers exploded. And when he collapsed before the finish, British officials helpfully aided his finish. When American Johnny Hayes came in an unassisted "second" in 2:55:18.4, he protested and was begrudgingly awarded gold.

Running along with New York City Marathon Winner *Shalane Flanagan*

"F**k yeah!" is what Shalane Flanagan shouted with a fist pump as she approached the finish line of the 2017 New York City Marathon. Well ahead of Kenya's Mary Keitany (who has won four times), Shalane became the first American woman to win the race in 40 years. With an Olympic silver medal, a marathon PR of 2:21:14, and several *New York Times* best-selling cookbooks (which she coauthored with Elyse Kopecky), Shalane knows a thing or two about finishing strong, and she is kindly sharing her thoughts with us.

Can you tell me a little about how you decided to run your first marathon after years of running shorter events?

I always knew I wanted to try the marathon, having grown up in the Boston area and having watched my dad run the Boston Marathon. I thought it was totally crazy. Insane! But at the same time, I was very intrigued and was like, "I want to be a part of that club." In 2008, after I won an Olympic medal for the 10,000M in Beijing, I was like, "Well, I guess I've reached the pinnacle of this event. Now what's the next big challenge?" And that was the marathon.

Can you describe what it felt like to win the New York City Marathon in 2017?

I'd been through a lot of highs and lows in the course of my marathoning career before I arrived at that moment, and I felt such a sense of delayed gratification and perseverance. I'd had moments where I felt like I should have done better for various reasons. The validation of overcoming an injury and just a lot of obstacles that made me doubt myself—I think that was my proudest moment because I overcame a lot of mental and physical barriers that could have derailed me very easily. I was just proud that I kept going for that goal.

How do you think your experience of winning compares to the average runner finishing?

I honestly don't think it's that different. I think that's why the marathon is so unique—because what casual runners are going through on the course is actually really similar to what I'm going through. To a certain degree, we experienced the same thing on the course that day. I could talk to someone who ran Boston 2018 [the marathon from hell that Des won], and we could have very similar stories.

Does it always feel good to finish, or are you ever disappointed?

The majority of the time, I feel disappointed to some degree unless I win. I feel like every elite runner is like that. We could have a PR day, but I guarantee everyone has one little critique of something they could have done better. But there is always a positive to finishing a race, to starting and completing something. You should always be proud of that effort.

Do you have certain mantras you use to push yourself through those last few miles?

Oh yes. Each race is different in what's important to me and how I want to execute. I'll never forget the Olympic Trials in 2012 to make my first Olympic team for the marathon. I find that I can get emotional toward the end. I don't know what it is, but I cry every single time I finish, and I could feel myself starting to get emotional, especially because making an Olympic team is such an honor. My mantra for that one was "cold execution." I just wanted to execute and not let my emotions overwhelm me in the moment to make sure I made the top three. Sometimes I say, "Why not me?" or "Why not today?" I've always used mental keys to get through.

As a professional marathoner, what is one tip or trick you would give a first-time marathoner?

Just embrace the fact that it's going to be very hard, but at the same time, crossing that finish line is life-changing. It's the best feeling. For a lot of people, it's transformative—becoming a marathoner and the journey over the course of those miles. It's similar to life—with all the highs and lows—embracing and leaning into the hurt and pain, but then rejoicing when you do feel well. I think there are so many teachable moments after you finish that you can draw upon and apply to your life. Just admit on the starting line that there are going to be moments of doubt and have some mental reasons why you're out there to draw upon in those tough moments.

Postrace

Congratulations! Welcome to the club! You ran a marathon and you've got the bumper sticker, medal, and inability to walk down stairs to prove it. Enjoy the day. Rest on your laurels. Brag to anyone and everyone (including the waiter taking your order for two helpings of queso). There is no better time to be alive than postmarathon—when you're living off euphoria and Gatorade, ready to devour anything and everything, and not quite feeling the brunt of your soreness.

But enough of that! Let's chat about what's next. Marathon legend Frank Shorter once said, "You have to forget your last marathon before you try another. Your mind can't know what's coming." I'll say from personal experience that it takes about six likes on an Instagram post, one burger, and all of an afternoon to forget just how bad the pain was and exclusively remember the glory of that last straightaway.

So, what are options for the future? You could run another marathon. There are so many wonderful races around the world (many of which are mentioned in this book). You could tackle a triathlon. The Ironman, especially, is a perennial favorite, although biking 100 miles has no appeal to me. There are also ultramarathons and trail marathons, which come in all shapes and sizes (Ryan Hall ran seven marathons on seven continents in seven days!).

Ultimately, though, whether you run 100 more marathons or hang up the sneakers, you should be extremely proud of what you've accomplished. You persevered through so many obstacles and can proudly say, "*I am a marathoner!*"

<< *Chicago Marathon, Illinois, USA, 2006*

BODY CHECK — Recovery

Your body has been to hell and back over the last 26.2 miles. Your muscles are sore, you're dehydrated, your body is low on fuel, and you're just plain tired. What's the best way to recuperate? Let's check in with some experts for one last body check.

Marathon coach Greg McMillan says there are some common mistakes finishers make. "A lot of runners mess up because they stop moving," he says. "They sit and they try to consume celebratory stuff when their GI system isn't ready for it, and then they get up and they're really stiff."

Let's start with the stiffness. I, on several occasions, have finished a marathon and thought, "I'm pooped. Let me just get in the car and rest." This, however, is not what those tired muscles need. Greg prescribes a combination of ice bath, hot shower, and walking around to keep those muscles loose. You'll be sore tomorrow no matter what, but you'll be nearly immobile if you spend the whole day sedentary.

With races often held on Sunday, there is the extra temptation to travel home after the race. I've taken trains, planes, buses, and automobiles on race day. If you can, take Monday off to give your body a day to recuperate before being locked in a seated position for extended hours. If you must travel, though, make sure to walk around as much as you can, whether in the plane's aisle or at a rest stop.

Greg also suggests taking some time before eating a big meal. Rehydrate yourself with a sports drink or a shake when you finish to start refueling, but wait a couple hours before your celebration feast.

What should you eat? Elyse Kopecky has some suggestions. "If it's a hot day, I usually don't crave a full meal right after I'm done running, so my go-to is the Can't Beet Me Smoothie from *Run Fast. Eat Slow*. Beets are really high in minerals and vitamins, so that's my immediate replenishment."

For something more solid, she says, "I love an egg scramble. I'll throw leftover roasted veggies—like sweet potatoes, mushrooms, zucchini, or onion—in a pan. I'll scramble up a couple eggs with some feta, and put an avocado on top."

"But," you say, "I want to celebrate! I just ran a freaking marathon!" Well, I have good news. Elyse also says, "I think the ultimate meal to celebrate after a marathon is a burger and a beer. A good-quality microbrew can be pretty hydrating after a run."

You heard it here, folks! A nutrition and running expert is telling you it's A-OK to sip a cold one to honor your accomplishment. ◼

How To Get the Best Marathon Photos

Picture or it didn't happen, right? You just ran 26.2 miles, the culmination of months' worth of hard training and sacrifice. You need to commemorate this moment with plenty of photos that you can post on social media and one day show your great-grandchildren. Here are all the best shots you'll want to get along the way.

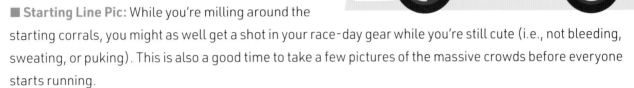

■ **Starting Line Pic:** While you're milling around the starting corrals, you might as well get a shot in your race-day gear while you're still cute (i.e., not bleeding, sweating, or puking). This is also a good time to take a few pictures of the massive crowds before everyone starts running.

■ **Midrace Selfie:** Mileage may vary here. Hardcore marathoners don't bring their phones on the course, and taking pictures could be potentially dangerous. But if you're careful not to run into anyone, snag a selfie in the back half of the first 13 so you're fresh but not too close to others.

■ **Photos from Friends:** If you've got friends at the race, tell them to take pictures and videos of you running by. You might look terrible and immediately instruct them to delete the photos postrace, but sometimes these action shots are the best ones.

■ **Professional Race Photos:** Most marathons have professional photographers on the course, and some races (like the Walt Disney World Marathon) have actual photo ops you can stop at. If you see a cameraperson, run toward them and smile. You can get these pictures online after the race.

■ **Finish Line Money Shot:** Most marathons also have plenty of cameras at the finish, so smile (or cry, it's up to you) as you run those last few feet to glory.

■ **Bite the Medal:** The "bite the medal selfie" is a marathon *classic*! You've got to do it no matter how gross you are. Capture the moment because you'll want to relive it.

■ **Marathon Backdrop Shot:** In the finishing area, there are often race-sponsored backdrops for photos with the race's name plastered on the side. They're very glamorous and professional as far as marathon pics go.

■ **Heat Shield Glory:** This is *the* photo to get. You're wearing your bib and your medal, with your heat shield wrapped around you. You're tired, but you're really happy. It's iconic and instantly recognizable. Bonus points if you can get a famous landmark in the background.

■ **All Cleaned Up:** After you've showered and put on fresh clothes, grab some additional pics with your medal. After all, the more pictures you get, the longer you can milk it on social media.

Navigating the Finish Festival

Ta da! You've finished your marathon, and now you're stumbling around like a sweaty zombie, clutching a hundred strange objects that volunteers are passing out. Where is your family? Where are the bathrooms? Did you finish the race only to die here? Possibly, but people just continue to shout, *"Keep moving!"* You're exhilarated and panting and smiling stupidly and totally lost. Well, here are some general tips for making the most of the postrace festival.

☐ **Medals:** They're usually giving these out first thing after finishing. Some wonderfully kind person will put it on you. It's OK to cry. I weepily embraced a Marine after he gave me my medal and saluted me in Washington, DC. Running 26.2 is an accomplishment, and that cannot be overstated.

☐ **Hydration:** Even if you're drinking at every aid station, you're going to need to hydrate at the finish. Often, they give out sports drinks or water bottles. Feel free to grab a couple because if you're like me, you'll chug the first one and still be thirsty two minutes later.

☐ **Food:** Most races also give out some kind of goody bag with food in it. There also might be bananas laying around somewhere. If someone is offering a bag, take it. As you stagger down this line, there could be more stuff and your hands will be full.

☐ **Heat Shields:** Someone will be passing out those tinfoil blanket things. I don't care how hot you are, take one. First, you'll get colder the longer you're outside and not running, so you might need it later. Second, it looks great in a picture. Tie it around your neck like a superhero cape or shove it in your bag, but don't skip it.

☐ **Keep Moving:** People are finishing behind you, so if at all possible, keep moving forward. If you have to stop, try to get over to the side so people can pass you.

☐ **Medical Stations:** There are swarms of medical personnel hovering around the finish. If you're feeling anything that doesn't seem right, flag one down. They've got medical stations set up, and they are there to help you. Never be afraid to ask for help.

☐ **Gear Check:** If you checked your gear at the start, you'll need to collect it now. Make sure you have some sort of reminder because plenty of people get swept up in the glory of finishing and leave their belongings at the race.

Meetup: Many runners don't carry phones with them during the marathon, so establish a meetup place before the race to reconnect with your family. The crowds are massive, and it can be a pain to find anyone otherwise. Some races have designated meetup spots, but even so, confirm with your friends ahead of time that you'll meet there. Don't assume anything.

Photos: Lots of races have little photo backdrops set up in the finish area where staff photographers are taking pictures with nice cameras. Get some pics. It may seem like a nuisance now, but you'll be glad you did it later when they're up on the website. Plus, your mom might get one put on a mug (speaking from personal experience).

Beer or Other Freebies: Many races have fun free extras for finishers, such as a glass of beer, a finisher shirt, or a pint of ice cream. Often, there will be a ticket on your bib that you'll have to exchange for the item so people don't take too much. Make sure you don't rip the ticket off before the race because then you're out of luck.

Bathrooms: There will be port-o-johns at the end of the race, but do you really want to celebrate by sitting in one of those? I always like to plan a bathroom stop into my postrace celebrations, so let everyone know you might need to head back to the hotel or pop into a restaurant for a little peace.

Postrace

Acknowledgments

There is no better place to start than with my agent, Danielle Svetcov. I am beyond lucky to work with you. Thank you for plucking me from obscurity and telling me I had what it takes to write a book. I will forever be indebted to you in so many ways. Your encouragement, intelligence, and humor are boundless. Also is there another human with more style? I think not!

To the team at Rizzoli, thank you, thank you, thank you for believing in *Marathoner* and giving me the opportunity to write it! I could not have asked for a better home for my first book. Thanks to Lori Malkin Ehrlich for taking the hundreds of blurbs and bits I wrote and arranging them into something so beautiful. Thanks to Candice Fehrman for gracefully editing my words and not laughing at me for misspelling *heel* so many times in a running book. Thanks to Jason Kayser for turning all my wild thoughts into illustrations and for sketching out multiple kinds of popsicles. Thanks to Victah Sailer for letting us comb through his thousands of marathon photos for all the great shots in the book. Thanks to Charles Miers for his excitement about and encouragement for this book. And, of course, thanks to Jim Muschett for steering the ship, for seamlessly building this book piece by piece, for answering emails so quickly, and for just being a wonderful person in general.

To all three of my publishing families, thank you for supporting me as a writer, as a runner, and as a friend all these years. Thanks to the team at Levine Greenberg Rostan for letting me eat more than my share of the office snacks and for telling me to quiet down far less often than you should. Special thanks to Sarah Bedingfield for our many breakfasts and your career advice, and to Victoria Skurnick, who can walk the length of Manhattan faster than I can run it. Thanks to the team at Jill Grinberg Literary Management for the truly life-changing internship and the friendships ever since. An especially *massive* thanks to Cheryl Pientka for encouraging me to run a marathon in the first place. Crazy to think where I'd be without you. And thanks to my new family at Curtis Brown Ltd., who welcomed me with open arms despite a mid-pandemic office move.

A very special thanks to the great Bridget Quinn for being a part of this book from the very beginning and through its various iterations. Thanks for being my marathon historian, and for being the only BQ I will probably ever be close to.

Also thanks to the wickedly talented Alyssa Dillon for designing my book proposal, cheering me on at marathons, geekily texting me about races, commiserating with me when we lose the New York City Marathon lottery on a yearly basis, and just being a genuinely incredible friend.

Thank you to everyone who allowed me to interview them for this book (and those who helped me set up the calls): Brinda Ayer, Bennett Beach (and Chris Lotsbom of the Boston Athletic Association), Amby Burfoot, Kate Carter, Dr. George Chiampas (and Alex Sawyer), Joe Connelly, Jim Crist, Lindsay Crouse, Dr. Mark Cucuzzella, Shalane Flanagan, Ryan Hall, Jim Heim (and Stuart Lieberman and Trina Singian), George Hirsch, Michal Kapral, Meb Keflezighi (and Merhawi Keflezighi and John Hricay), Elyse Kopecky, Des Linden (and Josh Cox), Greg McMillan, Amanda McGrory, Curt Munson (and Andy Marsh), Dave Obelkevich, Apolo Ohno, Danielle Quatrochi, and Kat Wang. You put the meat on the bones of this book, and I had such a blast chatting with each and every one of you.

Thank you to Kathy Annis, Dr. Janice Brown, Dr. Eric Potter, and Dr. Jennifer Scott for helping me become a better writer. And thank you a million times over to Ruthann Frederick for teaching me to write in the first place. My entire career and life is based on what you taught me in middle school, and you can tell your students that I don't go a day without mentally diagramming something as I write.

To all of my friends, I am extremely unworthy of you. Thanks to Beth Acta, Brandon Baker, Allison Cacich, Seann Cantatore, Bridget Carroll, Andrew Charney, Ben Colas, Lara Craine, Ashley Davis, Hannah Dupee, Spencer Dupee, Maggie Englehart, Paul Esposito, Brendon Farrell, Sean Flowers, Zach Gelfand, Paige Gormley, Sean Gormley, Sarah Grill, Michael Grosso, Ryan Hammond, Courtney Harstine, Cara Hartwig, Hallie Heald, Jen Holt, Peter Holt, Krista Huff, Sam Huff, Kyle Jones, Abby Kass, Vass Kazee, Jordan Kennedy, Shannon Krowicki, Victoria Krupa, Julie Kucks, Sarah Martinez, Sarah Menke, Kay Mollica, Hannah Muckle, Christa Price Murphy, Melissa Myers, Jackie Newman, Katie O'Hara, Cassandra Opper, Gracie Braatz Opper, Anupa Otiv, Bekah Parker, Olivia Potter, Sam Potter, Emily Raebek, Joel Richardson, Max Ross, Danielle Roth, Mel Rubin, Ryan Segedi, Emily Smicker, Victoria Snare, Alex Stedman, Samantha Stickle, Bethany Stumpf, Will Stumpf, Ryan Taggett, Jamie Tan, Dan Thelen, Joanna Tiger, Callie Troutman, Josh Troutman, Phoebe Tyers, Ciera Velarde, Caleb Vits, Danielle Von Lehman, and Sara Yoder for putting up with me.

Extra special thanks to those of you who have shown up and cheered for me at a race. Uncle Doodle, Aunt Elizabeth, Addie, the Fowlers, the Hilts (especially my best friend Kevin), Rob Polo, Shelby Boyer, Anne Vonk, BM Henderson, Aunt Barb and Uncle Steve, the Strongs, the Heinens, the Bedford/Millers, and Allison Arneberg—

you are all great. Thanks to Aunt Beth and Ryan for your help with this book as well. Josh Harstine and Hannah Ward, you earned special places in heaven for picking up my race bibs. #BBGTABT

Thank you to the baristas at R&R Coffee, The Bean, Foster, Starbucks, Laughing Man, Panera, Gregory's, Paper, Bluestone Lane, Joe and the Juice, Biggby, and Ground Central for letting me write and sip in your coffee shops for hours on end.

Thanks to all the extremely talented and interesting people behind *The A24 Podcast*, *Ali on the Run*, *Blank Check*, *Decoder Ring*, *Dissect*, *Fighting in the War Room*, *Heavyweight*, *Hurdle*, *Indiewire's Screen Talk*, *Little Gold Men*, *Podcast: The Ride*, *Post Show Recaps*, *Revisionist History*, *Rob Has a Podcast*, *Runners of NYC*, *The Toni Awards*, *Swiftish*, *This Had Oscar Buzz*, and *Who? Weekly* for providing plenty of listening content for marathon training. Same goes to Stephen King for his deliciously suspenseful audiobooks.

Thanks to the staff and volunteers at the Detroit, New Jersey, Marine Corps, Walt Disney World, Vermont City, Baltimore, Houston, and Chicago Marathons for creating such wonderful races to run.

Thanks to Grandpa for my writing genes and Grandma Janie for consistently reaffirming that pie is a suitable breakfast food. I miss you both loads. Thanks to Mimi and Papa for all the trips to Erma's and the John King Bookstore. Thanks to Danielle for just being an unrelenting force for good in my life. There has never been a better cousin to ride roller coasters with. Lava you.

Thanks to Jon, Daniel, and Janie for being slightly above-average younger siblings. All three of you deserve a Willkie button for your continued ability to put up with my shenanigans. Just remember that for as long as you live, it is my birthright to sit in the front seat of the car.

And last, and therefore most importantly, thank you Mom and Dad for literally everything. I could write a whole second book just on the things I owe you both for. A brief sample: cornflake cookies, a house to grow up in, movie theater popcorn, letting me be a writer instead of a doctor, socks, dental insurance, cheering me on at races, Slurpees, and never-ending love and support.

Page 236: Chiba Marathon, Japan, 2011 **Page 240:** *Boston Marathon, Massachusetts, USA, 2014*